Samuel Cunningham Kerr

The Jewish Church in its Relations to the Jewish Nation

Samuel Cunningham Kerr

The Jewish Church in its Relations to the Jewish Nation

ISBN/EAN: 9783337134778

Printed in Europe, USA, Canada, Australia, Japan

Cover: Foto ©Lupo / pixelio.de

More available books at **www.hansebooks.com**

THE JEWISH CHURCH

IN ITS

RELATIONS TO THE JEWISH NATION

AND TO

THE "GENTILES;"

OR, THE

PEOPLE OF THE CONGREGATION IN THEIR RELATIONS TO THE
PEOPLE OF THE LAND, AND TO THE PEOPLES
OF THE LANDS.

"Art thou a Master of Israel, and knowest not," that,
"Except a man be born again, he can not see the kingdom of God."

BY
Rev. SAM'L C. KERR, M.A.

CINCINNATI:
PUBLISHED BY WILLIAM SCOTT,
28 WEST FOURTH STREET.
1866

Entered according to Act of Congress, in the year 1866, by
REV. SAM'L C. KERR,
In the Clerk's Office of the District Court of the United States for the Southern District of Ohio.

PREFACE.

The late Dr. J. Addison Alexander, in his commentary on the Psalms, recently re-issued by the Presbyterian Board of Publication, translates the Hebrew phrase, *ben nekar*, in Ps. xviii, 44 (rendered in the common English version, "strangers") by the English phrase, "son of outland;" so, also, in his commentary on Isaiah (see Isa. lxii, 8). According to this rendering, Ex. xii, 43, referring to the ordinance of the passover, should read: *Any son of outland shall not eat of it.* The position is startling to the Bible student. If it be correct, how are we to understand Ex. xii, 48: "And when a *stranger* shall sojourn with thee and will keep the passover to the Lord, let all his males be circumcised, and then let him come near and keep it?" Again, if this position be correct, who were "the servants bought with money," or "thy bondmen and thy bondmaids of the *heathen* round about," who, it is acknowledged, were circumcised and ate the passover? If Alexander's rendering be correct, of course these renderings are incorrect.

The solving of this difficulty was the problem the author proposed to himself in the first place, without any thought of a work so extensive as the present. The first thing worthy of note that developed itself in the course of his investigations, was the fact, that our English translators had rendered indiscriminately a number of Hebrew words by a class of English words conveying the general idea of the term *stranger*. For a simple statement of the entire absence of any discrimination in the rendering of these Hebrew terms, see pages 16, 17. The next thing that developed itself, was, that the LXX were to a great extent uniform in rendering these Hebrew words into Greek, and in certain cases entirely so. In this extensive examination of the Greek translation, it became very apparent that there were two classes of *proselutoi*, corresponding entirely to the representations of Tradition respecting "the two sorts of proselytes"—the one being of *the people of the land*, the other being of *the people of the congregation*. Once understanding that these classes of *pro-*

selutoi were the proselytes of Tradition, some other rendering must be looked for of the expression "And when a stranger shall sojourn" (Ex. xii, 48), the "stranger" (*proselutos*) being of "the people of the land," who, upon being circumcised, came to be of "the people of the congregation." It was observed, also, that the Israelites in the land of Egypt, in our translation (Ex. v. 5) were called "the people of the land," and in the Septuagint (Ex. xxii, 21, and xxiii, 9) *proselutoi;* and that the LXX were careful never to render the Hebrew word rendered son of outland, or foreign born, by the Greek term *proselutos.* But the Israelites were not proselytes, in the common acceptation of the word, in the land of Egypt, neither were they sons of outland, or foreign born; but they were of "the people of the land," and *proselutoi*, or landborns, but not of Egyptian "stock" or lineage. So the *proselutoi* among the Hebrews were not sons of outland, or foreign born, but they were of "the people of the land," or landborns, and were of "stock" not "of Israel;" and when it was observed that the LXX had rendered, in Num. xv, 14, the verb rendered "shall sojourn" in Ex. xii, 48, by a Greek verb, which means "to be born again," and, in its connection, can only be so rendered, the whole difficulty seemed to be removed beyond a doubt—*the command,* "Any son of outland shall not eat of it" (the passover, Ex. xii, 43) *and the permission,* "And when a landborn shall be born again with thee and will keep the passover to the Lord, let all his males be circumcised, and then let him come near and keep it; and he shall be as *one that is born* (*azurah*) in the land" (Ex. xii, 48), *answering completely one to the other.*

Further examination developed even a worse confusion (see page 142), if possible, in the rendering of the Hebrew word, *azurah*, rendered, as above, "one that is born," and in the next verse, "homeborn." The expression, "*Azurah* among the children of Israel" (see Ez. xlvii, 22, and Num. xv, 29), in the connection used, settles the question that there was only a class among the children of Israel, or among those of "the stock of Israel," called *azurah.* Now, both *the clean* and *the unclean* of "the stock of Israel" were called He-

brews, or were of the Hebrew nation; but the one was only of the stock of the pious Eber, the other was not only of the stock, but of the religion of Eber—an Eberite of Eber, or a "Hebrew of the Hebrews."

It was observed again, that acts of a national character were performed in the name of "the people of the land" (see Chart, section II); and that "the seed of Israel separated themselves from the sons of outland" (Neh. ix, 2), and "separated themselves from the *peoples of the lands*" (Ez. ix, 1); and separated themselves from the *peoples* of the land (Neh. viii, 28), and God says, I "have separated you from *the peoples*" (Lev. xxii, 24). In our translation, the plural form of the original not having been preserved, the reader is at a loss to know whether the expressions, "people of the land" and "people," refer to the Jewish nation, or those from whom the Jewish nation must "separate themselves." The LXX carefully follow the Hebrew, in rendering a Hebrew plural by a Greek plural; and the author having corrected the Book of the Psalms and portions of the Prophecies, in this respect, *is assured of its great practical importance*—the plural "peoples," "peoples of the lands," etc., always referring to foreigners, or those of another nation.

At length, the way seemed open to indicate in a translation, in every instance, whether the person named was one of "the people of the congregation," "the people of the land," or "peoples of the lands;" or whether the person was a member of the Jewish Church, a citizen of the Jewish nation or a foreigner within the Jewish nation; and if a foreigner, whether of Jewish or foreign associations; and further, whether the person named was of Jewish lineage or "stock of Israel," or of Gentile lineage or "stock" not "of Israel." This translation has been made and subjected to the *severest conceivable test*—an exhaustive classification, showing the relation of the classes of persons one to the other, and to a variety of duties and privileges.

To accomplish this purpose, the classification, or Chart, as I have called it, has been divided into a number of Sections. The first Section (see page 45) is designed to classify the passages of Scripture upon which our conclusions are based, and

to lead the reader, step by step, in the most easy and practical manner, to a clear understanding of the relations of these classes of persons one to the other; and the reader would do well to prepare his mind *for the end to be reached*, by previously comparing page 67 with the last half of page 89. The remaining six sections are grouped together, proceeding, as in the last, from generals to particulars, so as to concentrate as far as possible *all the light* which the classification might develop in relation to these classes of persons and their privileges and duties.

The author feels the weight of the responsibility he assumes in making such an issue with our modern English translation in relation to the subjects treated of in this work—a translation which has been accepted so long as almost perfect. But if this translation, which has stood so long, is so venerable, much more venerable is that translation which our Saviour himself so often quotes (the Greek translation of the LXX, or the Septuagint); and when that translation concurs with the original Hebrew, it may well challenge our respect. The one was made when both the Hebrew and Greek languages were living languages, and by Hebrews who spoke both Hebrew and Greek; the other hundreds of years after the Hebrew and Greek ceased to be spoken languages—after a long night of literary and religious gloom, during which learning in any language had in a measure ceased to exist, and when the link that connected the past and the future was well nigh severed. In this dawn of the reformation and revival of literature was that translation made, which in our day it is reckoned almost sacrilege to question.

In the following pages the author is constrained to appeal to the original Hebrew, and the Greek translation, as referred to above, in reference to the matter in hand, against the confusion that exists in this modern translation. The Greek and Hebrew, so far as it seemed necessary to refer to them, are printed in English characters, as not so likely to confuse the common reader. The author is not tenacious of the terms he has selected to represent the original; indeed, if the matter were well understood, the terms in some instances, would

not be desirable, but for the present, they are sufficient, and represent substantially the original. He feels the more free to urge this matter upon Bible readers, inasmuch as others with himself see that the present rendering is in such a confused state, that it is "impossible for the English reader to attain to anything correct or satisfactory," in relation to the matter in hand.

The evidence which satisfied himself and others of this fact, is mostly contained in Chapters I and II, and the reasons which led to a different rendering are also stated in the latter part of Chapter II. Then follows the classification referred to above, setting forth, so far as could well be represented on paper, every variety of relation of these classes of persons one to the other, and the privileges and duties of each, as referred to in the Scriptures. Remarks are made on the classification in Chapters III, IV, V, and subjects are discussed from this new standpoint, briefly, but sufficiently, it is thought, to satisfy all that questions may be reached and settled which hitherto have defied solution. Some questions which, in the main, have divided large bodies of the modern Protestant Church are settled beyond a doubt (see foot note, page 156). The question of the so-called "Bible Servitude" or "Hebrew Slavery," the entering wedge to the solution of which is furnished by the rendering of Dr. Alexander, heretofore referred to, is shown to be an utter misconception. And the fact must be stated, that no progress was made until the key to this question was found and used, and when this was done, the solution followed rapidly and easily. The truth is, the *pure word*, as spoken by the Holy Spirit, has been rejected out of regard to the God-dishonoring conception that God approves, and has sanctioned, the buying and selling of one by the other of those "made of one blood." The confused rendering of Hebrew names, in the face of the distinctions preserved in the Greek translation, and the blotting out of distinctions made by the use of plural forms, as referred to in this work, were necessary to those who would read the Bible with this conception. In no other way could they assert that a foreigner, a son of outland, or one of "the peoples

of the lands" ever became one of "the people of the congregation." If there is any "chivalric" knight who can handle the Hebrew and Greek to sustain such a conception, we have prepared the way, and we *ask him to hie to the task!*

It is confidently believed, on grounds which can not here be indicated, that, besides these dividing issues which it is conceived are settled, still other questions which divide the modern Protestant Church, will find in this line of examination an easy solution. And I do not see much room for one to exult over another in what has been developed partly by *a mechanical logic.* Apropos to the easy solution (see foot note, page 156), of the issue with our Baptist brethren, I would say that if the rendering, "And when a stranger shall sojourn," etc., he came to be as "one that is born," or a "homeborn," or one "born in the country," be correct, the position of Prof. Knowles is correct; while if the person referred to under this name ("stranger"), was one of "the people of the land," who, upon being circumcised, came to be of the "people of the congregation," of course, his position is not correct. But the Professor or his friends need not be chagrined; they are no more responsible for the mistranslation than we are.

There are occasional repetitions, as to the reason and necessity of which, the author may have misjudged. In a matter of so much importance, it was thought that the main positions should be looked at in every possible light. To avoid a more frequent adoption of new terms, we have also frequently endeavored to express the idea by *quoting allusions.* The work is an attempt to correct an error which only could have occurred, seemingly, when the study of the Divine word was lost sight of in the subtleties of Aristotle. The stronghold of Error is yet in a Latin Bible, and we may well ask the question, have we yet entirely escaped the perversions of the Scholastic Theology of the middle ages?

If this work shall contribute to the removal of any causes of division among those who love the great "Master of Israel," and to a better understanding of the Divine Word and the extension of its influence; it will have accomplished its purpose. It is sent forth with this fond hope.

The author, upon a review of his work, especially of the first three chapters, has discovered many defects, both in want of clearness of statement and in order of arrangement, which, for the present edition, are beyond the reach of correction. Without previous experience in writing for the press, and having prepared it mainly amidst the arduous duties of a pastoral charge, and still more, in the endeavor to compress within the narrowest limits possible the singular incongruities of the English version which it was his object to point out, he found it difficult, at times, to make his statements satisfactory even to himself. But the intelligent reader, it is hoped, will not be at a loss to understand the author's meaning; and he asks at the hands of the critic, the indulgence due to a *pioneer* work.

I should do violence to my feelings if I should fail to attribute, under God, much of the success which I may have attained, to the surrounding influences of my *younger years*. To be born and reared in the pastoral charge of that eminent Bible expositor, the late Rev. Samuel Crothers, D. D., pastor of the Presbyterian Church, Greenfield, Ohio, and beyond him, to have had my first impressions of Bible truth from the occasional ministrations of neighboring ministers, such as the late Revs. James Dickey, Hugh S. Fullerton, Wm. Gage, and Wm. Dickey, *is no common lot*. To these names of " precious memory," allow me here to pay my mite of tribute. (For short memoirs of whom, see Wilson's Presbyterian Historical Almanac, for 1864.)

Acknowledgments are due to Dr. N. C. Burt, for his patient examination and valuable suggestions, almost from the commencement of the work; also to Dr. T. E. Thomas, for the same subsequently; also to Drs. E. D. MacMaster, W. C. Anderson, J. G. Monfort, for like services; and to my friend, Rev. J. M. Wampler, one of the Editors of the *Cincinnati Presbyter*, for valuable assistance in preparing the work for the press.

SAM'L C. KERR.

Fairmount, near Cincinnati,
　December 18, 1865.

CONTENTS.

CHAPTER I.

A statement of terms rendered Stranger in Ex. xii, 43-49, and in other passages—Confusion shown to exist. 13

CHAPTER II.

Evidences that the present rendering of Ex. xii, 43–49, is incorrect—Alexander's rendering—Inconsistencies—Conclusions foreshadowed—Inconsistencies resumed—Renderings of the LXX—Definitions.................... 24

CHART.

SECTION I.—ELEMENTARY........................... 45

SECTION II.— CITIZENS AND FOREIGNERS.—The Hebrew Nation—Commonwealth of Israel, or the People of the Land (made up of " Stock of Israel " and "Stock" not "of Israel"); and Aliens or Foreigners within the Commonwealth, viz.: Sons of Outland—Peoples of the Lands or Nations... 55

SECTION III.—LANDBORN AND LANDBORN BORN AGAIN.— "Stock" not "of Israel"—Consisting of the Landborn ("Thy Brother" whom "Thou shalt not hate") and the Landborn Born Again ("Thy Neighbor" whom "Thou shalt love as thyself")—the Ger and the Ger acting the Ger of the Hebrew, and the Proselutos and the Proselutos Pros. or Paroi., etc., of the LXX—"The Proselytes of the Gate" or " Habitation," and " Proselytes of Righteousness" of Rabbinical Tradition............. 62

Section IV.—Hebrew and Hebrew of the Hebrews.—
"Stock of Israel"—Consisting of "a Hebrew Man,"
("Thy Brother" whom "Thou shalt not hate") and a
"Hebrew of the Hebrews" ("Thy Neighbor" whom
"Thou shalt love as thyself")........................ 68

Section V.—Circumcision—Uncircumcision.—The Circumcised, Uncircumcised, and Uncircumcision....... 70

Section VI.—Sacrifices and Offerings.—The Positions in the previous Sections, as confirmed and illustrated in the Law of Sacrifices and Offerings, and in Tradition. 76

Section VII.—Remaining References.—Remaining References, and extent of the privileges of the Cities of Refuge... 84

CHAPTER III.

Who were Foreigners—"Aliens from the Commonwealth of Israel, and Strangers from the Covenants of Promise." 90

CHAPTER IV.

The Hebrew Nation—Commonwealth of Israel or People of the Land (see Chart, Sec. II)—made up "of stock of Israel" (see Chart, Sec. IV), and "of stock" not "of Israel" (see Chart, Sec. III)........................ 107

CHAPTER V.

Households of God..................................... 199

APPENDIX.

A—Proposed rendering of Ex. xii, 43-49.............. 231
B—The two Covenants................................. 232

COMMENDATIONS.

This is to say, that I have examined the manuscript treatise of the Rev. Mr. Kerr, on the subject of Membership in the Jewish Church, and that I think the results of his investigations are important to be made known to the public. He shows, by an exhaustive induction of the Scripture passages pertaining to the subject, that the law of the Ancient Church, as clearly exhibited both in the Hebrew Old Testament and the Septuagint Version, is clear and distinct, and that our translators, not having perceived the real significance of this law, have fallen into a confused rendering of the technical terms expressive of it, making it impossible for the English reader to attain to anything correct or satisfactory concerning it.

Mr. Kerr's exposition clears the subject of many difficulties, and leads to many conclusions of evident importance and permanent value.

N. C. BURT, D.D.,
Pastor Seventh Presbyterian Church, Cincinnati.

CINCINNATI, *May* 4, 1865.

Having perused the larger portion of the manuscript of Brother Kerr, with the accompanying Chart, I am of opinion, that he has rendered a very valuable service to Biblical interpretation; clearing up many difficulties, and throwing new light upon the constitution of the Old Testament Church, I cordially concur in the indorsement given by Dr. Burt.

THOS. E. THOMAS, D.D.,
Pastor First Presbyterian Church, Dayton, Ohio.

May 30, 1865.

So far as I can form a judgment, from the brief and cursory examination which I have been able to give, of the Rev. Mr. Kerr's work, on the subject of Membership in the Israelitish Church, I concur in the opinion expressed by the Rev. Drs. Thomas and Burt, of its value as a contribution to the interpretation of the Scriptures, on this interesting and important subject.

E. D. MAC MASTER, D.D., LL.D.

November 10, 1865.

We fully concur with Dr. Mac Master in the above.

W. C. ANDERSON, D.D.
J. C. MONFORT, D.D.

CHAPTER I.

A STATEMENT OF TERMS RENDERED STRANGER IN EX. XII, 43-9, AND IN OTHER PASSAGES — CONFUSION SHOWN TO EXIST.

43 And the LORD said unto Moses and Aaron, This is the ordinance of the passover: there shall no stranger (*kol ben nekar*) eat thereof:

44 But every man's servant that is bought for money, when thou hast circumcised him, then shall he eat thereof.

45 A foreigner (*toshabh*), and a hired servant shall not eat thereof.

46 In one house shall it be eaten; thou shalt not carry forth aught of the flesh abroad out of the house; neither shall ye break a bone thereof.

47 All the congregation (*gadath*) of Israel shall keep it.

48 And when a stranger (*ger*) shall sojourn (*yagur*) with thee, and will keep the passover to the LORD, let all his males be circumcised, and then let him come near and keep it; and he shall be as one that is born in (*azurah*) the land: for no uncircumcised person shall eat thereof.

49 One law shall be to him that is home-born

(*azurah*) and unto the stranger that sojourneth (*ger hgar*) among you.—(Ex. xii.)

In the above passage of Scripture, as rendered by our translators, we have the following expressions: There shall no *stranger* eat thereof (v. 43). A *foreigner* shall not eat thereof (v. 45). And when a *stranger* shall sojourn, etc., let him come near and keep it—the passover (v. 48). Our translators seem to have had serious difficulty in adjusting terms to translate this passage. If the words "stranger" and "foreigner," used here by our translators in rendering, the three Hebrew words, *ben nekar, toshabh*, and *ger*, distinguished between classes of persons in their day, the distinction is long since lost to us.

But did they distinguish? The rendering of *toshabh*, "foreigner," in the 45th verse, is a forced rendering, not occurring again in the Bible. It is rendered "stranger" twice, Lev. xxv, 6, 45. If this rendering be correct, then there shall no *stranger* eat thereof (43). A *stranger* shall not eat thereof (45). And when a *stranger* shall sojourn, etc., then shall he keep it (48). The distinction, which was one of sound, was made by giving the noun in the 45th verse a new and unheard-of meaning.

But, further, the Hebrew word rendered thus once "foreigner," and twice "stranger," is, with these three exceptions, the original wherever the word "sojourner" occurs in our English Bible. How then will this rendering strike modern ears? There

shall no *stranger* eat thereof (43). A *sojourner* shall not eat thereof (45). And when a *stranger* shall sojourn, etc., then he shall keep it (48). Did not a "stranger" sojourning become a "sojourner," and might not the "sojourner" eat the passover? We have the expression here, the *toshabh* (rendered " sojourner," wherever the word "sojourner" occurs in our English Bible)—*the sojourner shall not eat of it!* (43).

The original Hebrew may be read thus: Any son of *nekar* shall not eat of it (43). A *toshabh* shall not eat of it (45). And when a *ger yagur—ger will gurize* or *ger will act the ger* (whatever that may mean), then let him, etc. (48). The LXX (the Greek translation, which our Lord and his apostles so often quote), give these renderings of the above: Any *allogenēs* shall not eat of it (43). A *paroikos* shall not eat of it (45). And if any *prosēlutos proselthea* with you, etc. (48). I simply observe here, that both the Hebrew and Greek have three distinct words, all of which our translators attempt to render by the term "stranger," or its equivalent, most unaccountably reading "stranger shall sojourn," where the LXX read *prosēlutos proselthea*. The Hebrew word rendered stranger, in the 43d verse, is *ben nekar*, and is a cognate of *nokri* and the verb *nakar*, rendered " cut off," "cut off from his people"—made a *nokri*, a foreigner among his people. *Nokri* and *ben nekar*— *nokri and son of nokri*.

I. We remark: The Hebrew word *nokri*, which is generally rendered *allotrion* in the Septuagint, is rendered by our translators, "alien" (Deut. xiv, 21); "foreigner" (Deut. xv, 3); and "stranger" (Deut. xvii, 15). On three pages of a common-sized Bible, the same word in the original is translated by three different terms; the context showing no reason whatever for the change.

II. The whole expression *kol ben nekar* in the 43d verse is rendered in Ez. xliv, 9, and in Gen. xvii, 12, "any stranger;" and in this verse, and again in Ez. xliv, 9, by the expression "no stranger," the equivalent of "not any stranger;" while leaving off the adjective *kol*—"any," the expression *ben nekar* is rendered "stranger," Gen. xvii, 29, and the plural *benei nekar* is rendered "all strangers," Nehem. ix, 2; "sons of the stranger," Isai. lx, 10, and "sons of the alien," Isai. lxi, 5.

III. The word *toshabh* in the 45th verse, is rendered here and here only "foreigner;" in Lev. xxv, 6, and 45, "stranger," and then "sojourner," wherever that term occurs in our translation; in the Septuagint, *paroikos*, never *proselutos*.

IV. The word *ger*, rendered "stranger" in the 48th verse, is rendered "alien," Ex. xviii, 3. In Septuagint generally *paroikos* up to this chapter, but seldom afterward, and always *proselutos* when followed by the verb rendered "shall sojourn," and the participle

CONFUSION SHOWN. 17

"that sojourneth." In Ex. xii, 19—*geiōrais*; Isai. xiv, 2, *geiōras*.

V. The participle *gar* rendered "sojourneth" in the 48th verse, is rendered "dwelleth" in Lev. xix, 34, and by a noun (!) "strangers," 1 Chron. xvi, 19; Jer. xxxv, 7; Ps. cv, 12; Isai. v, 17.

VI. There is also another word, *zar*, rendered "stranger." See definition of the priest's household, Lev. xxii, 10-13; *zar*, "stranger," one of another household; also 1 Kings, iii, 17, 18. See Chap. V.

1. We have then (I) *nokri*—"stranger;" (II) *ben nekar*—"stranger;" (III) *toshabh*—"stranger;" (IV) *ger*—"stranger;" (V) the participle *garim*—"strangers;" and (VI) *zar*—"stranger."

2. We have again (I) *nokri*—"alien;" (II) *ben nekar*—"son of the alien;" (IV) *ger*—"alien."

3. We have (I) *nokri*—"foreigner;" and (III) *toshabh*—"foreigner."

4. We have (III) *toshabh*—"sojourner;" and (V) *gar*—"sojourneth;" the one not eating the passover (v. 45), the other eating it (48).

We have then these six words, each and every one meaning "stranger," and *yet they do not*, because four of them mean something else—three "alien" and the other "sojourner;" and yet one of these does not mean "alien," for it means "foreigner." If our translators distinguished between the words "foreigner," "stranger," "alien," "son of the stranger," "son of the alien," and even "sojourner" (the word ren-

dered "sojourner" is rendered "foreigner"), they have not indicated what word in the original means "stranger," what "foreigner," what "alien;" and not indicating it, they did not distinguish; and hence to them, as to us, these words only differed in sound but not in sense.

Now, is this translation, or only mystification? I have no hesitation whatever in saying that the original Hebrew word, without translation, "note or comment," would have been far preferable; and I would not to-day exchange my common English Bible, with the original Hebrew word, in every case, and generally the Greek rendering of the Septuagint, written on the margin, for all the commentaries in existence, and Gesenius' Hebrew Lexicon thrown in, so far as they throw light upon the five classes of persons which the Hebrews named *nokri, ben nekar, toshabh, ger, zar,* and the participle *garim* which our translators threw in, and rendered them all by the general name "stranger;" and the fact is, the name is too general for any one of them. What we might learn of these five classes of persons from what is said of them, *is entirely lost to us*, and yet if they all had been rendered uniformly by the term "stranger," it would not have been so bad; but to appear to distinguish by the several words "alien," "son of the alien," "stranger," "foreigner," and "sojourner," and yet not to distinguish, is really unpardonable. If these terms

were definite in our minds, and the Hebrew terms had an exact corresponding definiteness, the chances then would be twenty-five to one against our getting the correct meaning; but with these terms indefinite in our minds, and with these six Hebrew words rendered indiscriminately by so many indefinite terms, *what hope is there of our obtaining the true meaning?*

That the Hebrew words are definite, take the following: Ye shall not eat of anything that dieth of itself; thou shalt give it unto the stranger (*ger*) in thy gates that he may eat it; or thou mayest sell it unto an alien (*nokri*), Deut. xiv, 21. Here are three distinct classes of persons standing in a certain order of relation: *ye, ger* in thy gates, and *nokri*. But "every soul that eateth that which died of itself [among the *azurah* or among the *ger*], he shall both wash his clothes and bathe himself in water and be unclean until even" (Lev. xvii, 15). As it was lawful for the *ger* in thy gates and the *nokri* to eat it, it follows that the *ger* and *azurah* of Lev. xvii, 15, who upon eating it, should be unclean until even, were of the same class with *ye* of Deut. xiv, 21, who "shall not eat of that which dieth of itself." Then we have the three classes: *Ye*, forbidden to eat it, and the *ger* and *azurah* one of whom upon eating it, shall wash his clothes and bathe himself in water and be unclean until even, then he shall be clean. But if he wash them not nor bathe his flesh, then he shall

bear his iniquity (Lev. xvii, 15, 16). *Ye* and the *ger* and *azurah* were clean. But how did the *ger* come to be classed with the *azurah*? Turning to Ex. xii, 48, we read: And when a *ger yagur* (Septuagint *proselutos proselthca*)—when a *ger will act the ger*, let all his males be circumcised, and then let him come near and keep it, and he shall be as the *azurah;* so the *ger* classed with the *azurah*, and clean, was a circumcised *ger*, as only then he could be as the *azurah*—classed with the *azurah*.

Then we can distinguish at least three classes: (1) *Ye*, forbidden to eat, etc., the *ger* and *azurah* to whom it was unlawful—eating it were unclean, and not repenting and making the formal acknowledgment of repentance—*washing*—they were held to bear their sin. (2) The *ger* in thy gates who might eat it—evidently a class of persons unclean—impenitent. (3) The *nokri*, to whom they might sell—of whom they might exact usury (Deut. xxiii, 20)—of whom they might exact principal (Deut. xv, 3.) If we fail to distinguish these three classes of persons, as our translators do, what confusion follows: If you say, that which dieth of itself to the "stranger" you may sell it; I say, no, to the "stranger" you shall give it. If you say to the "stranger" you shall give it, and he may eat it; I say, no, the "stranger" that eats it is unclean. If you say, the "stranger" that eats it is unclean until even; I say, no, to the "stranger" you shall give

it, and he may eat; and if you say to the "stranger" you shall give it, I say, no, to the "stranger" you may sell; and thus one passage of Scripture is made to contradict another.

Take another example of a somewhat different character; the Hebrew word *toshabhim* (plural) is rendered in Lev. xxv, 45, "strangers;" give it the same rendering two verses below, and the 47th verse will read: And if a "stranger" or "stranger" wax rich by thee, and thy brother that dwelleth by him wax poor and sell himself unto the "stranger" or "stranger" by thee or to the stock of the "stranger's" family! It is said that there have been given to a certain passage in the New Testament some two hundred interpretations. This might easily be made to equal it. There is precedent for making it read, and if a "sojourner" or "stranger"—"foreigner" or "stranger"—"stranger" or "stranger"—"sojourner" or "alien"—"foreigner" or "alien"—"stranger" or "alien" wax rich by thee, and thy brother that dwelleth by him wax poor and sell himself unto a "stranger" or "sojourner"—a "stranger" or "foreigner"—a "stranger" or "stranger"—an "alien" or "sojourner"—an "alien" or "foreigner"—"alien" or "stranger" by thee, or to the stock of "stranger's"—"alien's" family.

Observing that the conjunction rendered "or" is usually rendered "and," then the first clause of the

verse would read "sojourner" and "stranger;" and further, observing that our translators supply the particle "or," in the second clause, so that it is most probably neither "and" nor "or," but should be read, the *ger*, a *toshabh*; and it can be seen that the number of interpretations that might be given this verse would be almost unlimited.

The Hebrew of this verse shows it to be manifestly a careful definition. Giving the connecting particle its usual definition it will read: And if a *toshabh* (from *yashabh* to dwell—*a dweller*) and *ger* (*proselutos*—Septuagint) wax rich by thee, and thy brother that dwelleth by him wax poor and sell himself unto the *proselutos*, a *dweller* by thee or to the stock of the *proselutos'* family, etc. A resident *ger*—a resident *proselutos* ("proselyte of habitation"), *is the person defined.* That a *ger* and *toshabh* was a brother, see verses 35–37.

In this same chapter you may have the following readings in the 40th verse: As a hireling and "sojourner," or "stranger" or "foreigner"—*your brother shall be with you as a foreigner!*

Look at this same verse in another phase. As a hireling and as a "sojourner" he shall be with thee. What does that mean? As a hireling and *toshabh* he shall be with thee. The *toshabh* and hireling shall not eat thereof (the passover, Ex. xii, 45). Who would suspect from our translation that the "foreigner" and hireling of Ex. xii, 45, and the

hireling and "sojourner" of Lev. xxv, 40, were the same classes of persons? Thy brother waxen poor and sold unto thee shall be with thee as the *toshabh* and hireling, *i. e.*, not eating the passover with thee. But as our purpose at present is not exposition, let this suffice. We have shown that there is confusion in our translation of *these words*, and that it works confusion, and is, in fact, a great obstacle in the way of our clear understanding of the Scriptures, *in matters in any way connected with these terms.*

CHAPTER II.

EVIDENCES THAT THE PRESENT RENDERING OF EX. XII, 43-49 IS INCORRECT—ALEXANDER'S RENDERING—INCONSISTENCIES—CONCLUSIONS FORESHADOWED—INCONSISTENCIES RESUMED — RENDERINGS OF THE LXX.—DEFINITIONS.

The Bible is the Word of God—is consistent with itself, and if we have a translation that is not consistent, in so far as it is not, we are sure that there is error in that translation. Of two things which are not consistent, one of them is not Bible truth.

(1) According to the rendering given to the Hebrew word *ben nekar*, by Dr. Joseph Addison Alexander, late Professor of the Presbyterian Theological Seminary at Princeton, New Jersey, the last clause of Ex. xii, 43, should read: Any son of outland shall not eat thereof (the passover). "The old word outland, which may still be traced in its derivative adjective *outlandish*, has been here employed to represent a Hebrew word for which we have no equivalent in modern English, and which means *foreign parts* indefinitely or collectively. The marginal version in the English Bible (sons of the stranger) is only an inexact approximation to the form of the original." (*Alexander on Ps.* xviii, 44-45;

see also on Isaiah, lxii, 8). Any son of *foreign parts—any born of the nations, within the limits of the nations, should he* (" sojourn ") *come among you—any emigrant* (except by special permission, the grandchild or third generation of an emigrant family of Edom, *thy brother*, or of Egypt, in whose land thou wast a *ger*, Deut. xxiii, 7, 8)—*any son of outland shall not eat of it* (the passover).

What becomes then of the translation of the 48th verse: " And when a stranger shall sojourn ?" etc. If Alexander be correct, the idea that a "sojourner" might ever lawfully eat the passover *is incorrect*.

In the 48th verse, " And when a stranger shall sojourn," etc., what did he become? I think all English readers of the Bible would say that a *stranger sojourning*, was simply a " sojourner," and the "sojourner" observing the law might eat the passover. Wherever the word " sojourner " occurs in our English Bible, the original is *toshabh* ; but a *toshabh* shall not eat thereof (Ex. xii, 45). *A sojourner shall not eat of it* (the passover)! That sentence is confounding to all my biblical predilections on this subject. If a " stranger sojourning," was not simply a " sojourner," how came there to be " sojourners " in the land? If he was simply a " sojourner," then the 45th verse is in direct conflict with the 48th—*they together containing a permission and a positive prohibition of one and the same thing.*

Again if we should call one born in our country a

"stranger," the expression could not be used concerning such an one: And when he (a "stranger") shall sojourn—come to dwell. The expression "And when a stranger shall sojourn," is only, strictly speaking, applicable to immigrant "foreigners,"—*sons of outland*, coming to dwell in our country. The expression, therefore, of Ex. xii, 48, "stranger shall sojourn," is only properly applicable to the foreign born; the very class which, according to Dr. Alexander's rendering, shall not eat of the passover under any circumstances whatever!

The children that are begotten of an immigrant Edomite, "thy brother," or Egyptian in whose land thou wast a *ger*, shall enter into the congregation (*khahal*, Heb. — *Ecclesia*, Septuagint) of the Lord, *only* in their third generation (Deut. xxiii, 7, 8). In Ps. xxii, 22, we read: "In the midst of the congregation (*khahal—ecclesia*) will I praise thee," quoted in Heb. ii, 12, where we read: "In the midst of the Church" (Greek, *ecclesia*). Guided by the last quotation, we read in Lev. xvi, 33, shall make an atonement *for all the people of the Church*. What consistency is there then with the above, in reading "And when a stranger shall sojourn"— when any foreigner shall come among the Jews, and be circumcised; then he may draw near and keep the passover, and, of course, be within the congregation — *khahal* — *ecclesia* — Church of the Lord?

Suppose he were an Edomite, or Egyptian of the first or second generation, what then?

"The seed of Israel separated themselves from the sons of outland"—*all emigrants* (Neh. ix, 2). "The people of Israel" separated "themselves from the *peoples* (plural in Hebrew and Septuagint) of the lands." "For they have taken of their daughters for themselves and for their sons; so that the holy seed have mingled themselves with the peoples (plural) of the lands," (Ezra ix, 1, 2).

Consider that *this nation* is *thy people*—so shall we be separated, I and thy people, from *every people* (Septuagint—*all nations*) which are upon the face of the earth (Ex. xxxiii, 13, 16).

(*a*) Then *all emigrants* were of the *nations—peoples of the lands—sons of outland*, and, among the Israelitish nation, were foreigners—and shall not eat of the passover.

(*b*) The people of the Hebrew nation—"commonwealth of Israel,"—were called "the people of the land." (See Chart, sec. II.) They were "of stock of Israel," and "stock" *not* "of Israel." The "stock" not "of Israel," are known in tradition as proselytes, and were of two classes; one circumcised, the other not, and were landborn children of emigrants —not born abroad, but born in the *holy land*, and, upon certain contingencies, were reckoned as of "the people of the land," of the Jewish nation and commonwealth.

(c) The people of the congregation (*khahal — ecclesia*) *the Jewish* church.

These classifications may be more briefly expressed thus: (a) The *peoples of the lands;* (b) *the people of the land;* (c) *the people of the congregation—Church;* or, (a) *The nations;* (b) *the nation* separate from the nations, from all *sons of outland—from peoples of the lands;* (c) and the covenant-keeping people of God, as a nation within a nation, which nation received additions only from that nation in whose bounds it existed.

The expression, rendered " stranger shall sojourn," (Ex. xii, 48), *ger yagur—ger will act the ger*, describes, not a *transition* between *nations* and *the* (Jewish) *nation*—*not a transition* between "the peoples of the lands" and "the people of the land," but a transition of one already of the Jewish nation to an *inner circle—* to the nation within the Jewish nation—a transition of one of "the people of the land " to " the people of the congregation "— *khahal — ecclesia —Church.* When a *ger will act the ger* (Ex. xii, 48), all the males to him being circumcised, etc.—*he did* not become one of " the people of the land "—did not become one of the Hebrew commonwealth or nation—was that already; but " he drew near and kept it" (the passover)—became one of " the people of the congregation "—the Jewish Church. The transition is between the two classes, called in tradition " proselytes of the gate," and " proselytes of

righteousness," both of which were of the "commonwealth of Israel"—the Jewish nation; the one circumcised and the other not circumcised. (See *Proselyte*, Cruden's Concordance, or any Bible Dictionary). The "proselyte of the gate" upon being circumcised became a "proselyte of righteousness." The Septuagint has no other rendering of *ger yagur* than *proselutos pros*. (See Ex. xii, 48; Num. ix, 14, xv, 14; Lev. xix, 34, xvii, 8; Ezekiel xiv, 7) and the expression *gor yagur*, rendered in Isaiah liv, 15, *shall surely gather*, is *proselutos pros*. in Septuagint! All the congregation (*gadath*, Septuagint, synagogue) of Israel shall keep it (the passover, Ex. xii, 47). The Septuagint has, "the whole multitude of the Church shall kill it" (the passover, Ex. xii, 6). The usual rendering of the words would give, the "whole Church (*khahal—ecclesia*) of the synagogue shall kill it."

I would suggest, as an approximation to the idea, the *whole witnessing Church or assembly of witness* shall kill it, corresponding somewhat to the different courts of the temple. There was (1) the court of the Gentiles (nations); (2) the court of the Jews (Jewish nation); (3) and the holy place—*sanctuary—tent, tabernacle of witness, or congregation*. The *peoples of the lands* entered no further than the *first;* the *people of the land* no further than the *second;* and *if the people of the congregation* did not worship in the tent of the congregation or sanctuary, the priests were

there, in some sense, their peculiar representatives or *mediators*.

I observe, that the blood of the sacrifices made on behalf of the *priest* and the *congregation* of Israel (Septuagint, synagogue) was put upon the horns of the altar of incense in the tabernacle or tent of the congregation (Lev. iv, 7, 18); while that of the *ruler* and *people of the land* (civil terms and offerings, perhaps, for civil offenses) was put upon the horns of the brazen altar in the court of the Jews— Jewish nation (Lev. iv, 25, 30). But I have *turned aside* thus briefly, to give a glimpse of what I hope to make plain in the following pages; and resuming, I repeat, with Alexander's rendering, made and published more than fifteen years ago, the whole *sojourning idea* must be abandoned.

Our translators were *compelled to abandon this idea*, or give the word, usually rendered "sojourner" (Heb. *toshabh*, Septuagint, *paroikos*) in this connection, a new and unheard-of meaning (the reading, a "sojourner" shall *not* eat of the passover, and "when a stranger shall sojourn," etc., *then he may, is too transparent*); and so they rendered it "foreigner" in the 45th verse, instead of the usual rendering, "sojourner," and preserved an appearance of correctness, and thereby their theory, and *only preserved it by such means.*

They resort to another expedient in Lev. xxv, 6, 45, and render this same word (*toshabh*, Hebrew—

paroikos, Septuagint) "stranger," to escape the expressions *sojourner that sojourneth,* and *children of sojourners which do sojourn.* What such a collocation of terms would mean, would be a question not easily answered. Only in these three instances do our translators depart from the usual rendering of the Hebrew word *toshabh;* and such a forced departure from the usual rendering in this vital point, the ordinance of the passover, *proves, conclusively,* that the common rendering of the word *toshabh,* by the term "sojourner," is incorrect — driven to read first "stranger" and then "foreigner," instead of "sojourner," *by a theory.*

You may render the Hebrew word *toshabh,* "sojourner," "stranger," "foreigner," and by as many more terms as you choose; yet it does not change the fact, that while the Jews read their law from year to year, century after century, that the class of persons which you designate by so many names, to them the name defined a class of persons outside the Jewish Church; and, I may say, not citizens of the Hebrew commonwealth. *They always read a toshabh shall not eat of it* (the passover, Ex. xii, 45).

Again, circumcision was the sign and seal of a covenant of promise "to you and your children," the token in their flesh of God's covenant with them as his people and his seal—God's pledge to him that kept the covenant, that God would fulfill the terms of that covenant, in making sure to him

the promises contained in that covenant; *that is*, a covenant relation was *proffered* " to you and your children "—" thou and thy seed after thee in their generations " (Gen. xvii, 9); and the man that kept the covenant in its requirements, was entitled to all promised in the covenant. God made a covenant with Abraham, and extended its privileges "to his seed after him in their generations "—*the Jewish nation only.* (See Chart, sec. VI.)

Again, if, the expression, " And when a stranger shall sojourn," etc. (Ex. xii, 48), describes a transition of one of the people of the land to the people of the congregation, then, of course, the expression, and when a son of outland " shall sojourn (come to dwell among you), let all his males be circumcised," etc., could never occur. *Such an expression never occurs in the Bible.* On the other hand, the Hebrew word *ger* in this connection, is always, in the Septuagint, rendered *prosēlutos;* and this Greek term is always, in the New Testament, rendered *proselyte;* if both these renderings are correct Ex. xii, 48, should read: And when a *proselyte* shall sojourn, etc. If Alexander is correct, the only person that could be said to " sojourn," *never did* — is never said to sojourn, in the Bible; on the other hand, if the rendering of the Hebrew word *ger* by the term *prosēlutos*, by the LXX, is correct, and if our rendering of that term in the New Testament is correct; then the proselyte—a person that could not be

said to sojourn, is the only person that is said to sojourn, in the Bible! *In short, the one that could, never did; and the one that could not, only did.* Hence, *again*, the action expressed in the verb in the 48th verse, rendered "shall sojourn," *being entirely out of place, is an incorrect rendering.*

Alexander's rendering utterly disjoints the present reading of the whole passage. Our translators must give the word *toshabh* in the 45th verse, an unheard-of meaning, to preserve a show of consistency in their rendering of the passage. Then *what does it mean?*

The ordinance they received *signifies regeneration.* For he is not a Jew which is one outwardly; neither is that circumcision which is outward in the flesh. But he is a Jew which is one inwardly, and circumcision is that of the heart, in the spirit and not in the letter, whose praise is not of men but of God (Rom. ii, 28, 29). The ordinance (circumcision) by the reception of which persons were formally admitted to the congregation, was expressive of more than the formation of a carnal relation. The Jew himself was "not a Jew who was only one outwardly;" "which say they are Jews and are not, but are of the synagogue of Satan." It was the distinctive token in their flesh, by divine appointment, of a peculiar people, whose heart prompted them to move in all their actions, out of regard to the praise of God rather than the praise of men. "For we are

the circumcision—*the regenerate*—which worship God in the spirit, and rejoice in Christ Jesus, and have no confidence in the flesh." The Bible defines circumcision as signifying regeneration, and its reception is the profession of such a state of heart, and thereby the receiver is formally united with God's people, just as baptism is a profession of our faith; and upon our receiving it, we are known as belonging to the Church. The ordinance of circumcision and baptism mean precisely the same thing—" the putting off the body of the sins of the flesh."

But let this suffice, and let us see what we have toward a new rendering.

The Hebrew of the expression, " stranger shall sojourn," in the 48th verse, is *ger yagur;* or, *ger will gurize;* better, *ger will act the ger* (whatever such an expression may mean). If *ger* means " stranger," then, according to the analogy of other languages, the idea ought to be conveyed in the expression, *when a stranger shall strangerize.* The Septuagint has *prosēlutos,* which has been rendered proselyte (see Acts xiii, 43); and then we would have—and when a proselyte *shall strangerize!*

But in one instance (Num. xv, 14), the expression, *ger yagur,* is rendered in the Septuagint *prosēlutos prosgenētai—pros,* " over and above," and *genētai,* " to be born." (See Donegan, or Liddell & Scott's Greek Lexicon.) And when a *ger—prosēlutos* shall

be born over and above—shall "be born again," etc.

It only remains to determine the meaning of the Hebrew word *ger*, which the LXX render, uniformly in this connection, by the term *prosēlutos*. The meaning is plainly inferable from the 43d verse. If "any son of outland shall not eat of it," you can have no other expression for those who might eat of it than *landborn;* and then we read, *any son of outland shall not eat of it* (43); *and* (48) *when a landborn shall be born again* upon receiving an ordinance expressive of a new birth—which is defined as meaning regeneration; then he shall draw near and keep it, for no uncircumcised *landborn* (*non- professing ger—prosēlutos*) shall eat of it.

Again, we get the meaning from the term *prosēlutos*, derived from the Greek verb *proserchomai*, which means, "come to you"—"your come" (see Liddell & Scott's Greek Lexicon); but "your come" *were by birth:*—a Moabite and Ammonite of the tenth generation, an Edomite and Egyptian of the third generation, were *your come by birth.* (See *Special Reasons*, Deut. xxiii, 3–8). And when such a *ger—prosēlutos, landborn*—shall be born again, all the males to him being circumcised—receiving the ordinance expressive of regeneration, then he was held as being in covenant, and in the *khahal*, *ecclesia*, *Church* of the Lord, and drew near and kept the passover. The emigrant—parent, children, grand-

children, and great-grandchildren—all who came into the holy land, were *sons of outland*, of the *peoples of the lands*—"of the nations who shall not enter thy congregation"—*khahal—ecclesia—Church*— "visiting the iniquity of the fathers upon the children, unto the third and fourth generation of them that hate me" (Ex. xx, 5)—all emigrants of image-worshiping nations "bare their iniquity" —shall not enter thy congregation; but not so their children, "which they begat in your land" (Lev. xxv, 45). Such children were *proselutos*, "your come by birth in your (holy) land," and under your protection—government (*ger*, *proselutos in thy gates*), were called "the people of the land," and upon their own voluntary act (*ger yagur*) declaring, or professing a new birth, and receiving an ordinance defined as meaning regeneration, they became one of the *people of the congregation—Church of the Lord.*

The LXX then mean, in rendering the Hebrew word *ger* by the Greek word *proselutos, your come by birth in your land* (full expression) *in thy gates* under your government—separated unto your nation, having no *dealings* with the nations or peoples of the lands.

Upon the law given in respect to the Edomites and Egyptians, viz.: "Thou shalt not abhor an Edomite, for he is *thy brother;* thou shalt not abhor an Egyptian, because thou wast a *ger* in his land;

the children that are begotten of them shall enter into the congregation — *khahal—ecclesia—Church—* of the Lord in the third generation;" I observe that Israel having been a *ger* in the Egyptians' land, and Edom (Esau and Jacob were brethren) and Israel being brethren, in a remote sense, the former held a relation to Israel approaching to that of brother who might enter the congregation (observe not every *brother* might enter the congregation); and hence the third generation, the grandchildren of such emigrants were not held as *sons of outland* (see Ex. xii, 43) or "peoples of lands;" and being joined to Israel—taking the oath of allegiance, as we would say—and although born abroad, yet for the reasons given, were treated as landborn—*ger—prosĕlutos*, and such a *ger*, upon being born again and circumcised, entered the congregation and kept the passover. All the congregation of Israel shall keep it (Ex. xii, 47).

I here draw an inference: Israel being a *ger* in the Egyptians' land and a *brother* of the Edomite, were considerations of equal force — each might " enter the congregation of the Lord in their third generation." To the first and second generation—the non-privileged of Edom—the term *brother* was applied; but the being a *ger* in the Egyptians' land, was a consideration of equal force. The Egyptian was to be treated as the Edomite, "thy brother," who was even called a brother before the third

generation, and certainly the title should not be denied to the third generation of each in the land, to one of whom it had been applied previously, and to the other a term equivalent to the term "thy brother." And when a *ger* (who was a brother) *yagur—will act the ger*, etc. (Ex. xii, 48)—a *prosēlutos*—" your come by birth in your land," *shall be born again*, etc.

By the law given in respect to the Moabites and Ammonites, "An Ammonite or Moabite shall not enter into the congregation — *khahal* — *ecclesia* — *Church*—of the Lord, even to their tenth generation shall they not enter into the congregation—*khahal*—*ecclesia*—*Church*—of the Lord forever: Because they met you not with bread and water in the way when ye came forth out of the land of Egypt, and because they hired against thee Balaam the son of Beor of Pethor of Mesopotamia, to curse thee. Nevertheless the Lord thy God would not hearken unto Balaam; but the Lord thy God turned the curse into a blessing unto thee, because the Lord thy God loved thee. *Thou shalt not seek their peace nor their prosperity all thy days forever*" (Deut. xxiii, 3–6). I observe that this last injunction, *shall not seek their peace*, was that "commanded by the prophets" concerning the *peoples of the lands—nations*, and therefore emigrant Moabites and Ammonites were held, for ten generations, as belonging to the nations—as *peoples of the lands;* and although many of them

were born in the (holy) land, they were held as sons of outland, and such never entered the congregation of the Lord. The people of the congregation were made up of the people of the land (landborn), and those reckoned as such. "And now, O our God, what shall we say after this? for we have forsaken thy commandments, which thou hast commanded us by thy servants the Prophets, saying, the land unto which ye go to possess it, is an unclean land with the filthiness of the *peoples* (plural) *of the lands* (Septuagint, *peoples of nations*); with their abominations which have filled it from one end to another with their uncleanness. Now, therefore, give not your daughters unto their sons; neither take their daughters unto your sons, *nor seek their peace nor wealth forever* (Ezra ix, 10–12). The then existing generations of Israel ("all thy days forever") shall *not seek their peace nor prosperity* (Moab and Ammon), even of their children, which "they begat in your land," "to their tenth generation."

The line of positive prohibition then ran as follows:

All emigrants were "peoples of the lands," from whom "the people of Israel separated themselves" (Ez. ix, 1), *sons of outland* who shall not eat of it (the passover, Ex. xii, 43), from whom "the seed of Israel" "separated themselves" (Neh. ix, 2), and who themselves are represented as complaining, "The Lord hath utterly separated me from his people" (Isai. xlvi, 3). All these were of the na-

tions — "Gentiles," *not* of the Jewish nation, "aliens from the commonwealth of Israel and strangers from the covenants of promise," under that dispensation; to whom were no *covenant* promises, they were a *people not my people.* "For she hath seen that the heathen—*nations* (Hebrew, *goyim*, Septuagint, *ethnea*) entered into her sanctuary whom thou didst command, that they should not enter into thy congregation" (Hebrew, *khahal*, Septuagint, *ecclesia*)—*Church* (Lam. of Jer. i, 10).

Except (*a*) for special reasons, as above, the third generation of an emigrant family of Egypt or Edom, *were not held* as "peoples of the lands"—"sons of outland"—"utterly separate"—not held as of a foreign nation, but it was commanded that "the children begotten of them shall enter the congregation (*khahal—ecclesia—Church*) of the Lord in their third generation" (Deut. xxiii, 8); *shall* (be permitted to) *enter in their third*, etc.

Except (*b*) for special reasons, as above, an emigrant family of Moab and Ammon and their children, even " which they begat in your land," *were held* as " sons of outland," " peoples of the lands." (Compare Deut. xxiii, 6, and Ezra ix, 10–12.) They were held as sons of outland of whom, to the tenth generation, it was commanded, as of the nations (Lam. i, 10), that they shall not enter the congregation (Hebrew, *khahal*, Septuagint, *ecclesia—Church*)

of the Lord (Deut. xxiii, 3); *shall not* (be permitted to) *enter till their tenth*, etc.

Except (*c*) it would seem that the Canaanites, whom Israel was required to destroy, were to be held in greater *abhorrence* than even Moab and Ammon (hence the expression, "nations round about"—Lev. xxv, 44—not of those nations in whose land Israel dwelt); if so, they *bare their iniquity*—their seed were to be held in *perpetual abhorrence* by Israel under that dispensation. Of them (the seven nations), "thou shalt save alive nothing that breatheth" (Deut. xx, 16); while they might make peace with the cities *very far off* from them, which are not of the cities of these [seven] nations (Deut. xx, 10, 15). Solomon asks God to hear the prayer of the *nokri* that comes from a *far off country* (2 Chron. vi, 32; 1 Kings viii, 41). When "the iniquity of the Amorite was full," they would seem to have been given over to Satan.

Finally: I observe further, upon the word *yagur* (Ex. xii, 48), that we have no word the equivalent of this, in modern English—as Dr. Alexander observes, in selecting the old word, outland, to represent the Hebrew word *nekar*—nor have we the counterpart of the word outland in the word *landborn* (*ger*), free from objections. I therefore only attempt an approximation. And when a *ger—prosēlutos* (brother in a national sense—born within

the nation, and therefore in a sense a child of the nation), *yagur—will act the ger* (none but a *ger* acted the *ger*—it was the peculiar privilege of one born in the holy land—within the nation, to whom was proffered a covenant relation—to hold that relation, declare a new birth, and receive an ordinance—" a token in their flesh of a covenant relation")—*will act* in reference to the privileges to which by birth he is entitled—claim his birthright—the privilege of covenanting with Jehovah—when "your come" by birth, as thus defined, shall " be born again"— when a *ger will act the ger* (a tree is known by its fruits, men are to be known by their actions); the landborn comes forward and declares his desire to enter into covenant with Jehovah; and upon receiving that ordinance which means regeneration, then he was to be held as in covenant with God, by his own act, and it was a token in his flesh of " the covenant betwixt me and you," a sign to him of duties to be done, and a " seal" which, those duties done, God would ever acknowledge as the seal of his covenant, and the bearer entitled to the promises of that covenant. Upon thus doing and thus formally binding himself in covenant by his own act, every male to him being circumcised, then shall he draw near and keep it, and he shall be as the " Hebrew of the Hebrews" of the land (not homeborn—they were both homeborn and " born again;" but one was " of the stock of Israel," the

other of the stock of the nations—*Gentile stock, or lineage*); for no uncircumcised (*ger—prosēlutos—brother*) shall eat thereof (Ex. xii, 48).

Briefly, then, I have indicated what I hope to make plain in the *following Chart* and annexed pages; and I ask the indulgence of my readers, in my attempt to travel a path little trodden in modern times, for all imperfections of style, poverty of expression, and the peculiar phraseology adopted, which, in my view, was necessary to the proper presentation of the subject, owing to the want of equivalents in the English language, with which to give the force of the original.

CHART.

SECTION I.—ELEMENTARY. *

	Wall of Partition	
2. And this is the manner of the release; every creditor that lendeth aught unto his *neighbor* shall release it: he shall not exact it of his *neighbor* or of his *brother*, because it is the Lord's release............		..3. Of a foreigner (Heb. *nokri*, Sept. *allotrion*)...............
...thou mayest exact it again, but that which is thine with thy *brother*, thine hand shall release (Deut. xv).		
19. Thou shalt not lend upon usury to thy *brother*, usury of money, usury of victuals, usury of any thing that is lent upon usury........................		..20. Unto a stranger (Heb. *nokri*, Sept. *allotrion*)...............
...thou mayest lend upon usury, but unto thy *brother* thou shalt not lend upon usury; that the Lord thy God may bless thee in all that thou settest thine hand to in the land whither thou goest to possess it (Deut. xxiii).		[Ittai the Gittite and Ruth the Moabitess were *nokri* and *nokriah*, which words in these and ten or twelve other instances, the LXX render *xenos* and *xenea*—

* The object of the following Chart is to separate and show the relations of *three classes of persons*, which the Hebrews called " the people of the congregation," " the people of the land," and " the peoples of the lands." The general plan is to place in opposite columns the names which designate persons as belonging to particular classes, and what is said of them, and where it seemed necessary, these are *italicized*. Where two classes are spoken of in the same connection, the transition of the narrative from one column to another, is indicated by *leaders or dotted lines*.

15. Thou shalt in any wise set him king over thee, whom the Lord thy God shall choose; one from among *thy brethren* shalt thou set king over thee: thou mayest not set [over thee......................

25. If thou lend money to any of *my people* that is poor by thee, thou shalt not be to him as a usurer; neither shalt thou lay upon him usury (Ex. xxii).

7. I rebuked the nobles, and the rulers, and said unto them, ye exact usury, every man of his *brother* (Neh. v).

7. In thee have they set light by father and mother; in the midst of thee have they dealt by oppression with the stranger—*ger*—*proselutos:* in thee have they vexed the fatherless and widow.

12. In thee have they taken gifts to shed blood; thou hast taken usury and increase, and thou hast greedily gained of thy *neighbors* by extortion, and hast forgotten me, saith the Lord God.

23. *The people of the land* have used oppression and exercised robbery, and have vexed the poor and needy; yea they have oppressed the stranger—*ger*, *proselutos*—wrongfully (Ez. xxii).

•

4. And if *the people of the land* do any ways hide their eyes from the man, when he giveth of his seed unto Molech, and kill him not:

5. Then I will set my face against that man, and against his family, and will cut him off, and all that go a whoring after him, to commit whoredom with Molech, from among their people (Lev. xx).

Neighbors—brothers—my people—people of the land —ger—proselutos.

25. What thinkest thou Simon? Of whom do the kings of the earth take custom or tribute? Of their own children or..

..26. Peter saith unto him..

---

xenoi, from the covenants of promise (Eph. ii, 12).]
...a stranger (Heb. *nokri*, Sept. *allotrion*), *since he is not thy brother*]—(Deut. xvii).

2. The seed of Israel separated themselves from all strangers—*benei nekar* (Neh. ix).

1, 2. Have not separated themselves from the *peoples of the lands* —holy seed have mingled themselves with the *peoples of the lands;* taken their daughters for themselves and sons —the hand of the princes hath been chief in this trespass (Ez. ix).

26. Nevertheless even him (Solomon) did *outlandish* (Heb. *nekarioth*, Sept. *allotriai*) women cause to sin (Neh. xiii,).

3. The Lord hath utterly separated me (*ben nekar*) from his people (Isai. lvi).

[Hence, Dr. Alexander renders *ben nekar*, son of outland—son of foreign parts. (See Alex. on Ps. xviii, 44, 45; also, on Isai. lxii, 8)].

Son of outland—peoples of the lands—foreigners and *strangers (xenoi) from the covenants of promise.*

...*of allotrion?*..............

.. *of allotrion*............

SECTION I.—ELEMENTARY. 47

... Jesus saith then are the children free (Matt. xvii).

Children.

35. [And if *thy brother* (a *ger* and *toshabh*, Sept. *proselutos* and *paroikos*), a "proselyte of habitation," wax poor and his hand faileth with thee, then thou shalt relieve him that he may live with thee].

36. Take thou no usury of him or increase; but fear thy God; that *thy brother* may live with thee.

37. Thou shalt not give him thy money upon usury, nor lend him thy victuals for increase (Lev. xxv).

[That a *ger—proselutos* was a *brother*, see page 37. There are two classes, plainly distinguishable here among the *children* or *brothers*, as opposed to ..

... viz.; *thou* and the *ger* and *toshabh* ("proselyte of habitation"); and the former must relieve the latter, and not lend to him upon usury; but he might lend to the foreigner upon usury. (See above.) Hence the *ger* and *toshabh* was not a foreigner, but yet a distinct class from *thou*].

Thou.

43. Now when the congregation (synagogue, Greek) was broken up, many of the Jews and religious *proselutoi* followed Paul, etc. (Acts xiii).

33. And he shall make an atonement for the holy sanctuary, and he shall make an atonement for the tabernacle of the congregation, and for the altar, and he shall make an atonement for the priests, and *for all the people of*

"Proselyte of Habitation."

Foreigners.

... the *nokri* of the Hebrews, or *allotrion* of the Greeks....................

Foreigner.

46. Then Paul and Barnabas waxed bold, and said, it was necessary that the word of God should first have been spoken to you: but seeing ye put it from you, and judge yourselves unworthy of everlasting life, lo, we turn to the Gentiles (*Ethn. nations*).

47. For so hath the Lord commanded us, saying, I have set thee to be a light of the Gentiles (*Ethn. nations*) that thou shouldst be

[The Middle Wall of Partition.]

[Clean and Unclean.]

Jews and religious proselutoi.	Unclean — irreligious proselutos.	Gentiles or Nations.
the congregation (Heb. *khahal*, Sept. *ecclesia*)— *Church* (Lev. xvi).	That which dieth of itself to the *ger*—Sept. generally *proselutos*—in thy gates you shall give it and he may eat it (Deut. xiv, 21).	for salvation, unto the ends of the earth. 48. And when the Gentiles (*Ethn. nations*) heard this, they were glad (Acts xiii).
Ye shall not eat of anything that dieth of itself; thou..................	.. shalt give it unto the stranger—*ger* — in thy gates, that he may eat it, or..........	.. mayest sell it unto an alien (Heb. *nokri*, Sept. *allotrion*), for...... ....
.. thou art a holy people (Deut. xiv, 21). Thou	*Ger* — *proselutos in thy gate*—"*proselyte of the gate.*"	*Nokri—allotrion—for-eigner.*
CLEAN. 15. And every soul that eateth that which died of itself [among the *azurah*, or among the *ger*], he shall wash his clothes and bathe himself in water, and be unclean until even (Lev. xvii). The *ger — proselutos*, ("proselyte of righteousness") classed with the *azurah*.	**UNCLEAN.** 48. And if a stranger shall sojourn —*ger yagur* —*ger will act the ger*, cross the line between the *clean* and *unclean*. The LXX render once *proselutos prosgnetai* (Num. xv, 14). Hence, And if a *ger—proselutos*, landborn shall "be born again," all the males to him being circumcised, then (he shall cross the line between the *clean* and *unclean*) he shall draw near and	*Ben nekar*, "sons of outland," — emigrants, parents, children, grandchildren, and great-grandchildren — "third and fourth generation of them that hate me." Except (1), Canaan was reprobated (cup of her iniquity was full), to the latest generation, Except (2), Moab and Ammon were to be treated *as ben nekar*, to the tenth generation. (See Deut. xxiii, 3, 4.)
.... keep it (the passover), and he shall be as the *azurah* (Ex. xii). Hence the *ger* classed with the *azurah*, as above, was the re-		

(column divider labels: *Clean and Unclean.* | *The line between Clean and Unclean.* | *Middle Wall of Partition.*)

generated, circumcised ger—proselutos, or land-born born again.

49. One law shall be to the *azurah* and to the *ger hgar—ger that acts the ger* in your midst (Ex. xii).

Because you were......

Gar or *garim — one acting the ger*—none but a landborn is said to be born again.

34. As the *azurah* of you so shall be the *ger* that acts the *ger* with you, and *thou shalt love him as thyself*;............

Thou shalt love thy neighbor as thyself (royal law). (Lev. xix, 18.)

That eats shall be unclean.

(Ger) and *toshabh, hgar* — resident landborn born again (Lev. xxv, 6).

The Line between Clean and Unclean.

....

.. "thy brother," in a limited sense, already. (Jacob and Esau were brethren.)

. a *ger—landborn* in the Egyptians' land; born and grew up together in the same land, and therefore not strictly . .

5. And Pharaoh said the *people of the land* are many, and ye make them rest from their burdens (Ex. v).

. . for ye were *gerim* (plural) (*proselutoi*. Sept.) in the land of Egypt (Lev. xix).

Thou shalt not hate *thy brother* in thine heart (Lev. xix, 17).

Ger—proselutos--"your come by birth in your lands"—landborn.

Between the so-called "proselytes of the gate" and "proselyte of habitation," I know of no distinction, unless one dwelt *in thy gates* (walled towns); the other in the country or villages.

Mayest give and may eat.

"Proselyte of habition," *ger* and *toshabh* (resident landborn — *thy brother* Lev. xxv, 35–37).

The Middle Wall of Partition.

Except (3), Edomite and Egyptian to the third generation.

Because Edom is......

....

. . *ben nekar*—"sons of outland," one to the other—had mingled as a people. (See Deut. xxiii, 7, 8.)

Thou shall not *seek their peace nor prosperity* all thy days forever —Moab and Ammon to their tenth generation (Deut. xxiii, 6).

Nor *seek their peace or their wealth forever*; —peoples of the lands (Ez. ix, 11, 12).

To this mayest sell.

Toshabh (resident foreigner) *shall not eat* the passover (Ex. xii, 45).

Neighbors.		Brothers.		Foreigners.
Ger hgar.		*Ger.*		*Nokri,* Hebrew.
Proselutos proskeim. or *proselth.* or *prosporeu* etc. Nation within a nation.		*Proselutos.* Nation.		*Allotrion,* Greek of the Sept. Nations.
The people of the congregation.		The people of the land.		The peoples of the lands
Landborn, born again.		Landborn.		Sons of outland.
Born of the Spirit.		Born in the land.		Born abroad.
	Clean and Unclean.		Middle Wall of Partition.	THIS SHALL NEVER;* 43. Any son of outland shall not eat of it (the passover)............
THIS SHALL KEEP, ...47. All the congregation (Heb. *gadath,* Sept. synagogue) of Israel shall keep it...............		.... WHEN THIS WILL DO, ETC., THEN ..48. And when a *ger* —*proselutos* — landborn (brother) shall be born again† and will keep the passover to the Lord, let all his males be circumcised, and then let him..............		A *dweller,* resident *foreigner* (*toshabh,* Hebrew — *paroikos,* Sept.) shall not eat of it (Ex. xii, 45)
HE SHALL KEEP, ...come near and keep it, and he shall be as the Hebrew of the Hebrews of the land.........		UNTIL HE DO, NEVER, ... for no uncircumcised *ger* — *proselutos*— landborn (brother) shall eat thereof...............		[Now, therefore (the Middle Wall of Partition being broken down) ye are no more strangers *xenoi* ("*xenoi* from the covenants of promise") and *paroikoi* —dwellers (resident foreigners), but fellow-citizens with the saints, and of the household of God, Eph. ii, 12, 14, 19.]
....49. One law shall be to the Hebrew of the Hebrews and to the landborn born again in your midst (Ex. xii).				

* Logic of "the law of the passover" *traced in small capitals.*

† The expression, *ger will act the ger,* represents the original better; the man becoming a *ger* by birth in the land and choice of associations, could become a member of the congregation by his own act, the ordinance he received declaring the state of his heart.

SECTION I.—ELEMENTARY. 51

22. And it shall come to pass, that ye shall divide it by lot for an inheritance unto you, and to the strangers that sojourn (*gerim hgarim* Heb., plural—*proselutois tois paroikousin*, Sept.—to the landborn who are born again) among you, which shall beget children among you: and they shall be unto you as the *azurah*—Hebrew of the Hebrews—among the children of Israel; they shall have inheritance with you among the tribes of Israel.

23. And it shall come to pass, that in what tribe the stranger sojourneth (*ger gar*, Heb.—*proselutoon en tois proselutois*, Sept.—the landborn is born again—the ger acts the ger) there shall ye give him his inheritance, saith the Lord God (Ez. xlvii).

[But every servant of a man (Ex. xii, 44) "bought for money"]—WHO? *So far as such servants were not of Abraham's seed*..................

The line between Clean and Unclean.

....

.. do act the ger with you — are born again with you..... ....

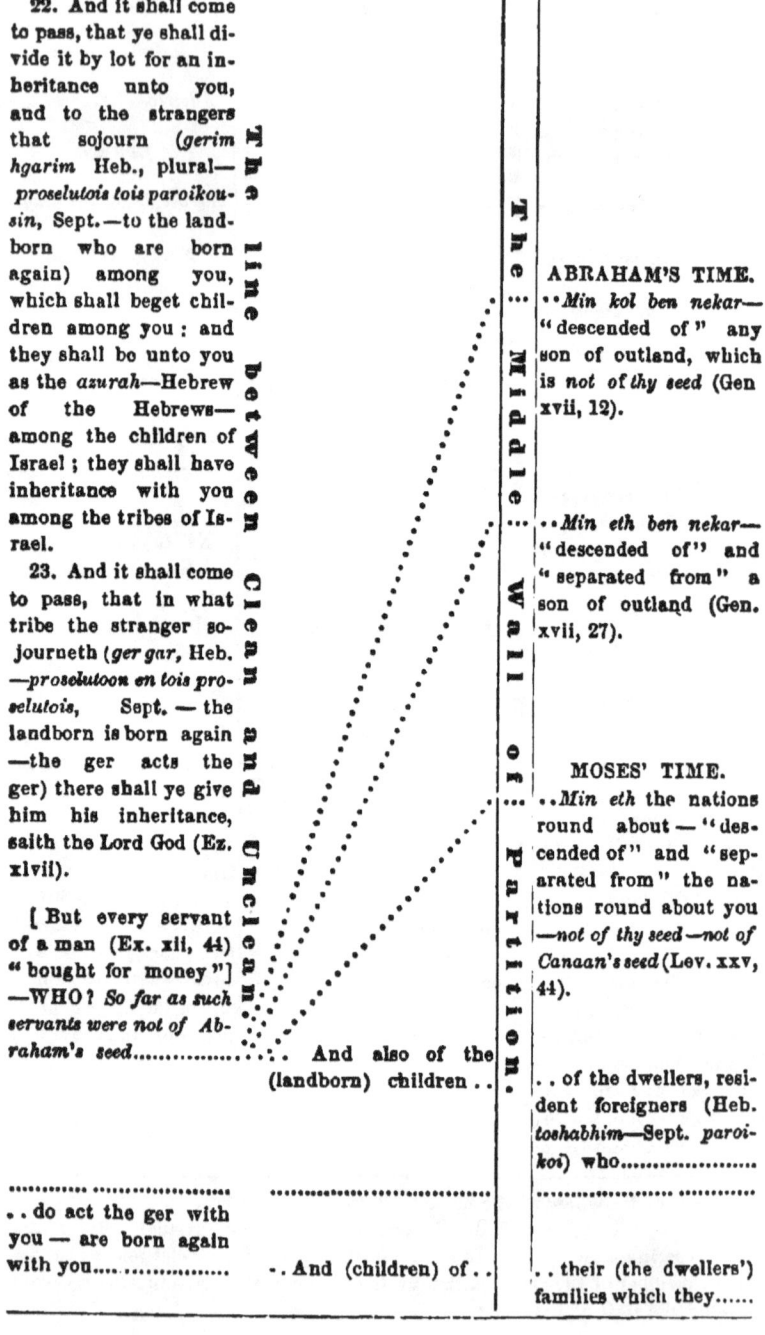

.... And also of the (landborn) children ..

....

.. And (children) of ..

The Middle Wall of Partition.

... ABRAHAM'S TIME.
..*Min kol ben nekar*—"descended of" any son of outland, which is *not of thy seed* (Gen xvii, 12).

... ..*Min eth ben nekar*—"descended of" and "separated from" a son of outland (Gen. xvii, 27).

... MOSES' TIME.
..*Min eth* the nations round about — "descended of" and "separated from" the nations round about you—*not of thy seed*—*not of Canaan's seed* (Lev. xxv, 44).

.. of the dwellers, resident foreigners (Heb. *toshabhim*—Sept. *paroikoi*) who..................
....

.. their (the dwellers') families which they......

....	.. begat in your land, Lev. xxv, 45, (who	[The renderings, given in this column, on the previous page, are the only renderings that can be given, so that those renderings shall be consistent with the following declaration on this page :]
.. do act the ger with you — are "begotten again" with you)— " when thou..... .... " let him come near and keep it, and he shall be as (the children of) the Hebrew of the Hebrews of the land........ .... "The children of promise were counted for the seed." " If children (of promise), then heirs." [And ye yourselves shall make them inherit among " your children " after you ... and over, *your brethren*, the children of Israel, ye shall not rule one (Israelite) over another (Israelite) with rigor, Lev. xxv, 46.] Taking the oversight, .. not for filthy lucre, neither as being lords over God's heritage (1 Pet. v, 2, 3); for one is your master even Christ and all *ye are brethren* (Matt. xxiii, 8). The Church is *God's heritage*, and he who led it in the wilderness leads it now; and *then*, as *now*, one is your master, even Christ, and *all ye are brethren ! !* .... household, in Israel by receiving the ordin-	.. hast circumcised him then " 'Ex. xii, 44)..... .... for no uncircumcised (*ger — proselutos —* landborn) shall eat of it," (the passover, Ex. xii, 48). [The *ger* in thy gates was an unclean person (Deut. xiv, 21). The hireling whose wages shall not remain with thee over night .. of the *ger* in thy gates (Lev. xix, 13 ; Deut. xxiv, 14), upon being born again, and united with	*Kol ben nekar*—Any son of outland shall not eat of it (the passover, Ex. xii, 43). The seed of Israel separated themselves from the sons of outland (Neh. ix, 2), and the people of Israel from the peoples of the lands (Ezra ix, 1). Heathen — *nations* (round about) entered into her sanctuary, whom thou didst command that they should not enter into thy congregation (*khahal*, Heb. —*ecclesia*, Sept.)— Church (Lam. i, 10). A dweller, resident foreigner (Heb. *toshabh* —Sept. *paroikos*) shall not eat of it (the passover, Ex. xii, 45).

(Vertical column labels: The line between Clean and Unclean. | Middle Wall of Partition.)

SECTION I.—ELEMENTARY. 53

ance of circumcision at the hands of the head of that household, became a servant "bought with money" in that household—a child of the Spirit but not of the flesh—a proper child of a spiritual household.]

8. And when Asa heard these words, and the prophecy of Oded the prophet, he took courage, and put away the abominable idols out of all the land of Judah and Benjamin, and out of the cities, which he had taken from mount Ephraim, and renewed the altar of the Lord that was before the porch of the Lord.

9. And he gathered all Judah and Benjamin, and the strangers (*garim*, Heb.—they who act the ger—*proselutous tous paroikonntas*, Sept.—landborn born again) with them out of Ephraim and Manasseh, and out of Simeon: for they fell to him out of Israel in abundance, *when they saw that the Lord his God was with him* (2 Chron. xv).

6. But they said, we will drink no wine; for Jonadab the son of Rechab our father commanded us, saying, Ye shall drink no wine, neither ye, nor your sons for ever.

2. And David commanded to gather the strangers (*gerim—proselutous*, plural — landborns) that were in the land of Israel, and he set masons to hew wrought stones to build the house of God (1 Chron. xxii).

17. And Solomon numbered all the strangers (*gerim—proselutous*—landborns) that were in the land of Israel, after the numbering, wherewith David his father had numbered them; and they were found a hundred and fifty thousand and three thousand and six hundred.

18. And he set threescore and ten thousand of them to be bearers of burdens, and fourscore thousand to be hewers in the mountain, and three thousand and six hundred overseers to set the people a work (2 Chron. ii).

18. For the Scripture saith, Thou shalt not muzzle the ox that treadeth out the corn. And, the laborer is worthy of his reward (1 Tim. v).

The line between Clean and Unclean.

The Middle Wall of Partition.

Unclean.		Wall of Partition.
7. Neither shall ye build house, nor sow seed, nor plant vineyard, nor have any; but all your days ye shall dwell in tents; that ye may live many days in the land where ye be strangers (*garim*, *ger acters* — landborn born again, Jer. xxxv). 17. Then shall the lambs feed after their manner, and the waste places of the fat ones shall strangers (*garim*, *who act the ger—landborn born again*) eat (Isa. 5).	13. Woe unto him that buildeth his house by unrighteousness, and his chambers by wrong; that useth his neighbor's service without wages,* and giveth him not for his work (Jer. xxii).	

Clean.

* Was the temple built by unrighteousness, its chambers by wrong? Any one of these one "hundred and fifty thousand and three thousand and six hundred" *gerim*, Heb.—*proselutous*, Sept.—landborns whose wages as a *sakeer* it was unlawful to retain over night (Deut. xxiv, 14) might become more than a *sakeer—hireling*.

The head of a family—a ger upon acting the ger, all his males being circumcised (Ex. xii, 48), received an *inheritance* in the tribe in whose bounds he professed regeneration (Ez. xlvii, 23). See Chap. IV.

An individual—a ger upon acting the ger, and being united to a household by the reception of the sign of a perpetual covenant.—"When thou hast circumcised him" (Ex. xii, 44), became a servant (*Miqnath keseph*) in a household, and had his *inheritance* in the family where he professed regeneration. (See Lev. xxv, 46; also Chap. IV.)

SECTION II.—CITIZENS AND FOREIGNERS,

The Hebrew Nation—Commonwealth of Israel, or the People of the Land (made up " of Stock of Israel" and " Stock" not "of Israel"); and Aliens or Foreigners within the Commonwealth, viz.: Sons of Outland—Peoples of the Lands or Nations.

The Middle Wall of Partition.

....that is not of *thy people Israel*, but cometh out of a far country for thy name's sake.

42. For they shall hear of thy great name, and of thy strong hand, and of thy stretched out arm; when he shall come and pray toward this house.

43. Hear thou in heaven thy dwelling place, and do according to all that..

......as do *thy people Israel;* and that....................

13. And when Athaliah heard the noise of the guard and of the people, she came to the people into the temple of the Lord.

14. And when she looked, behold, the king stood by a pillar, as the manner was, and the princes and trumpeters by the king, and all *the people of the land* rejoiced, and blew with trumpets. And Athaliah rent her clothes, and cried, Treason, treason!

17. And Jehoiada made a covenant between the Lord and the king and the people, that they should be the Lord's people; between the king also and the people.

18. And all the *people of the land* went into the house of Baal, and brake it down; his altars and his images brake they in pieces thoroughly, and slew Mattan the priest of Baal before the altars. And the priest appointed officers over the house of the Lord.

41. Moreover, concerning a stranger (*nokri*, Heb. — *allotrion*, Sept.).........................

.. the stranger (*nokri— allotrion*) calleth to thee for; that all *peoples of the earth* may know thy name, to fear thee,......

.. they may know that this house which I have builded, is called by thy name.

53. For thou didst separate them from among all the *peoples of the earth*, to be thine inheritance, as thou spakest by the hand of Moses thy servant, when thou broughtest our fathers out of Egypt, O Lord God.

60. That all the *peoples of the earth* may know that the Lord is God, and that there is none else (1 Kings viii).

19. And he took the rulers over hundreds, and the captains, and the guard, *and all the people of the land;* and they brought down the king from the house of the Lord, and came by the way of the gate of the guard to the king's house. And he sat on the throne of the kings.

20. And all the *people of the land* rejoiced, and the city was in quiet: and they slew Athaliah with the sword beside the king's house (2 Kings xi).

5. And the Lord smote the king, so that he was a leper unto the day of his death, and dwelt in a several house. And Jotham the king's son was over the house, judging the *people of the land* (2 Kings xv).

23. And the servants of Amon conspired against him, and slew the king in his own house.

24. And the *people of the land* slew all them that had conspired against king Amon; and the *people of the land* made Josiah his son king in his stead (2 Kings xxi).

30. And his servants carried him in a chariot dead from Megiddo, and brought him to Jerusalem, and buried him in his own sepulchre. And the *people of the land* took Jehoahaz the son of Josiah, and anointed him, and made him king in his father's stead (2 Kings xxiii).

3. And on the ninth day of the fourth month the famine prevailed in the city, and there was no bread for the *people of the land.*

19. And out of the city he took an officer that was set over the men of war, and five men of them that were in the king's presence, which were found in the city, and the principal scribe of the host, which *mustered the people of the land,* and threescore men of the *people of the land* that were found in the city (2 Kings xxv).

......Samaria, knew not the manner of the *God of the land;* therefore he hath sent from among them, and behold, they slay them, because they know not the manner of the *God of the land* (2 Kings xvii. Read from verse 24 to 41, same chap.).

Period of Division — Middle of the

1. But king Solomon loved many strange (*nokr.—allotr.*) women, together with the daughter of Pharaoh, women of the Moabites, Ammonites, Edomites, Zidonians, and Hittites.

2. Of the *nations,* concerning which the Lord said unto the children of Israel, Ye shall not go in to them, neither shall they come in unto you; for surely they will turn away your heart after their gods: Solomon clave unto these in love—*unto those women* (or *wives*) *of the nations.*

8. And likewise did he for all his *strange* (*nokr. — allotr.*) wives (1 Kings xi).

["Strange wives "— always wives of *nokr.,* Heb.—*allotr.,* Sept.]

26. Wherefore they spake to the king of Assyria, saying, The *nations* which thou hast removed, and placed in the cities of.................
....

25. And they transgressed against the God of their fathers, and went a whoring after the gods of the *peoples of the land,* whom God destroyed before them (1 Chron. v).

SECTION II.—CITIZENS AND FOREIGNERS. 57

......which is not of *thy people Israel*, but is come from a far country for thy great name's sake, and thy mighty hand, and thy stretched-out arm; if they come and pray in this house:

33. Then hear thou from the heavens, even from thy dwelling-place, and do according to all that......

......as *doth thy people Israel*, and may know that this house which I have built is called by thy name (2 Chron. vi).

13. And she looked, and behold, the king stood at his pillar, at the entering in, and the princes and the trumpets by the king; and all the *people of the land* rejoiced, and sounded with trumpets; also the singers with instruments of music, and such as taught to sing praise. Then Athaliah rent her clothes, and said, Treason, treason!

17. Then *all the people* went to the house of Baal, and brake it down, and brake his altars and his images in pieces, and slew Mattan the priest of Baal before the altars—(*all the people* are here said to do what *all the people of the land* are said to do in 2 Kings xi, 18).

20. And he took the captains of hundreds, and the nobles, and the governors of the people, and all the *people of the land*, and brought down the king from the house of the Lord; and they came through the high gate into the king's house, and set the king upon the throne of the kingdom.

21. And all the *people of the land* rejoiced; and the city was quiet, after that they had slain Athaliah with the sword (2 Chron. xxiii).

21. And Uzziah the king was a leper unto the day of his death, and dwelt in a several house, being a leper; for he was cut off from the house of the Lord: and Jotham his son was over the king's house, judging the *people of the land* (2 Chron. 26).

25. But the *people of the land* slew all them that conspired against king Amon; and the *people of the land* made Josiah his son king in his stead (2 Chron. xxxiii).

The Middle Wall of Partition.

32. Moreover concerning the stranger (*nokr.—allotr.*)..............

.. the stranger (*nokr.—allotr.*) calleth to thee for; that all *peoples of the earth* may know thy name, and fear thee,. ..

13. Know ye not what I and my fathers have done unto all the *peoples of the lands;* were the gods of the *nations* (*goyim—Ethn.*) of those lands any ways able to deliver their lands out of my hand? (2 Chron. xxxii).

1. Then the *people of the land* took Jehoahaz the son of Josiah, and made him king in his father's stead in Jerusalem (2 Chron. xxxvi).

19. Nevertheless, *the people* refused to obey the voice of Samuel; and they said, Nay, but we will have a king over us; that we also may be like........ ..all the *nations—goyim—Ethn.* (1 Sam. viii).

24. And Samuel said to *all the people*, See ye him, whom the Lord hath chosen, that there is none like him among *all the people?* And *all the people* shouted, and said, God save the king (1 Sam. x).

.. Molech, he shall surely be put to death; the *people of the land* shall stone him with stones.

3. And I will set my face against that man, and will cut him off from among his people; because he hath given of his seed to Molech, to defile my sanctuary, and to profane my holy name.

4. And if the *people of the land* do any ways hide their eyes from the man, when he giveth of his seed unto Molech, and kill him not;

5. Then I will set my face against that man, and against his family, and will cut him off, and all that go a whoring after him, to commit whoredom with Molech, from among their people (Lev. xx).

47. Thou therefore gird up thy loins, and arise, and speak unto them all that I command thee; be not dismayed at their faces, lest I confound thee before them.

18. For behold, I have made thee this day a defenced city, and an iron pillar, and brazen walls against the whole land, against the kings of Judah, against the princes thereof, against the priests thereof, and against the *people of the land* (Jer. i).

19. The princes of Judah, and the princes of Jerusalem, the eunuchs, and the priests, and all the *people of the land*, which passed between the parts of the calf;

20. I will even give them into the hand of their enemies, and into the hand of them that seek their life; and their dead bodies shall be for meat unto the fowls of the heaven, and to the beasts of the earth (Jer. xxxiv).

27. The king shall mourn, and the prince shall be clothed with desolation, and the hands of the *people of the land* shall be troubled (Ezek. vii).

28. And the rest of the people, the priests, the Levites, the porters, the singers, the Nethinims, and

The Middle Wall of Partition.

24. So the children went in and possessed the land, and thou subduedst before them the inhabitants of the land, the Canaanites, and gavest them into their hands, with their kings, and the *peoples of the land*, that they might do with them as they would.

30. Yet many years didst thou forbear them, and testifiedst against them by thy Spirit in thy prophets: yet would they not give ear; therefore gavest thou them into the hand of the *peoples of the lands* (Neh. ix).

SECTION II.—CITIZENS AND FOREIGNERS. 59

all they that had separated themselves from the..... | ..*peoples of the land*.....
....
......unto the law of God, their wives, their sons, and their daughters, every one having knowledge, and having understanding.

29. They clave to their brethren, their nobles, and entered into a curse, and into an oath, to walk in God's law, which was given by Moses the servant of God, and to observe and do all the commandments of the Lord our Lord, and his judgments and his statutes.

30. And that we would not give our daughters unto the.. | ...*peoples of the land*......
....
......nor take their daughters for our sons.

31. And if the... | ..*peoples of the land*..
....
......bring ware or any victuals on the Sabbath day to sell, that we would not buy it of them on the Sabbath, or on the holy day; and that we would leave the seventh year, and the exaction of every debt (Neh. x).

23. In those days also saw I Jews that had married wives of Ashdod, of Ammon, and of Moab.

24. And their children spake half in the speech of Ashdod, and could not speak in the Jews' language, but according to the language of *people*........ | ...*and people.*

26. Did not Solomon, king of Israel, sin by these things? yet among many nations was there no king like him, who was beloved of his God, and God made him king over all Israel; nevertheless even him did.. | ...outlandish (*nokr.—allotr.*) women cause to sin.

30. Thus cleansed I them from all..................... | ...strangers—*nekar.—allotrioxeos — foreignness* — foreign connections or associations (Neh. xiii).

17. And in every province, and in every city, whithersoever the king's commandment and his decree came, the Jews had joy and gladness, a feast and a good day. And many of the *peoples of the*

The Middle Wall of Partition.

2. The Jews gathered themselves together in their cities throughout all the provinces of the king Ahasuerus, to lay hand on such as sought their hurt; and no man could withstand them; for the fear of them fell upon...

21. And the children of Israel, which were come again out of captivity, and all such as had separated themselves unto them from the filthiness of the......

1. Now, when these things were done, the princes came to me, saying, The people of Israel, and the priests, and the Levites, have not separated themselves from..

2. For they have taken of their daughters for themselves, and for their sons; so that the *holy seed* have mingled themselves with.........................
....yea, the hand of the princes and rulers hath been chief in this trespass.
3. And when I heard this thing, I rent my garment and my mantle, and plucked off the hair of my head, and of my beard, and sat down astonished (Ezra ix).

land became Jews; for the fear of the Jews fell upon them (Esther viii). —[Or as the Sept. has it: And many of the *nations* were circumcised and judaized, (or acted as Jews), through fear of the Jews.]

.. *all peoples* (Esther ix).

.. heathen (*goyím--Eth.*) *nations* of the earth (Ezra vi).

.. *the peoples of the lands*, doing according to their abominations, even of the Canaanites, the Hittites, the Perizzites, the Jebusites, the Ammonites, the Moabites, the Egyptians, and the Amorites.
.. *the peoples of lands* ..
....

11. Which thou hast commanded by thy servants, the prophets, saying, The land unto which ye go to possess it, is an unclean land with the filthiness of the *peoples of the lands*, with their abominations, which have filled it from one end to another with their uncleanness.

14. Should we again break thy commandments, and join in affin-

SECTION II.—CITIZENS AND FOREIGNERS. 61

	The Middle Wall of Partition.	
		ity with the *peoples of these abominations?* wouldest not thou be angry with us till thou hadst consumed us, so that there should be no remnant nor escaping? (Ezra ix)
2. And Shechaniah the son of Jehiel, one of the sons of Elam, answered and said unto Ezra, We have trespassed against our God, and have taken..		. strange (*nokr.* — *allotr.*) wives of the *peoples of the lands*
11. Now therefore make confession unto the Lord God of your fathers, and do his pleasure and separate yourselves from................................		..the *peoples of the land* and from *nokr.*, *allotr.* wives (Ezra x).
2. The seed of Israel separated themselves from all..		.. strangers —*benei nekar*—"sons of outland" (see Alexander on Ps. xviii, 45; also Isai. lxii, 8)............... ....
......and stood and confessed their sins and the iniquities of their fathers (Neh. ix).		Any (*ben nekar*) "son of outland" shall not eat of it (the passover, Ex. xii, 43).

SECTION III. — LANDBORN — LANDBORN BORN AGAIN.

"Stock" not "of Israel"—Consisting of the Landborn ("Thy Brother" whom "Thou shalt not hate") and the Landborn Born Again ("Thy Neighbor" whom "Thou shalt love as thyself")—the Ger and the Ger acting the Ger of the Hebrew, and the Proselutos and the Proselutos Pros. or Paroi., etc., of the LXX— "The Proselytes of the Gate" or "Habitation," and "Proselytes of Righteousness" of Rabbinical Tradition.

[47. And if a *landborn* and *dweller* (resident landborn—"proselyte of habitation") wax rich by thee, and thy brother that dwelleth by him wax poor and sell himself unto a *landborn, a dweller* by thee or to the stock of the landborn's family—Lev. xxv.]

[35. And if thy brother, a *landborn and dweller*, be waxen poor, and fallen in decay with thee: then thou shalt relieve him: that he may live with thee.]

36. Take thou no usury of him, or increase; but fear thy God, that thy brother may live with thee.

37. Thou shalt not give him thy money upon usury, nor lend him thy victuals for increase (Lev. xxv).

9. Also thou shalt not oppress a *landborn*, for ye know the heart of a *landborn*, seeing ye were landborn in the land of Egypt—Ex. xxiii.

4. And the king of Egypt said unto them, Wherefore do ye, Moses and Aaron, let the people from their works: get you unto your burdens.

5. And Pharaoh said, Behold, the *people of the land* now are many, and ye make them rest from their burdens (Ex. v).

18. He doth execute the judgment of the fatherless and widow, and loveth the *landborn*, in giving him food and raiment.

19. Love ye therefore the *landborn*; for ye were *landborns* in the land of Egypt (Deut. x).

11. And thou shalt rejoice before the Lord thy God, thou, and thy son, and thy daughter, and thy

Middle Petition.

7. Send thine hand from above: rid me, and deliver me out of great waters, from the hand of strange children (*benei nekar*—sons of outland).

11. Rid me, and deliver me from the hand of strange children (*benei nekar*—sons of outland), whose mouth speaketh vanity, and their right hand is a right hand of falsehood (Ps. cxliv).

[Then shall stand strangers (*zarim*, see Chap. V.) and feed your flocks, and the *children of outland* (*benei nekar*—plural) shall be your

man-servant, and thy maid-servant, and the Levite that is within thy gates, and the *landborn*, and the fatherless, and the widow, that are among you, in the place which the Lord thy God hath chosen to place his name there.

14. And thou shalt rejoice in thy feast, thou, and thy son, and thy daughter, and thy man-servant, and thy maid-servant, and the Levite, the *landborn*, and the fatherless, and the widow, that are within thy gates (Deut. xvi).

5. They break in pieces thy people, O Lord, and afflict thy heritage.

6. They slay the widow and the *landborn*, and murder the fatherless.

7. Yet they say, the Lord shall not see, neither shall the God of Jacob regard it.................

17. Thou shalt not pervert the judgment of the *landborn*, nor of the fatherless, nor take the widow's raiment in pledge:

18. But thou shalt remember that thou wast a bond-man in Egypt, and the Lord thy God redeemed thee thence; therefore I command thee to do this thing.

19. When thou cuttest down thy harvest in thy field, and hast forgot a sheaf in the field, thou shalt not go again to fetch it; it shall be for the *landborn*, for the fatherless, and for the widow; that the Lord thy God may bless thee in all the work of thy hands.

20. When thou beatest thine olive-tree, thou shalt not go over the boughs again: it shall be for the *landborn*, for the fatherless, and for the widow.

21. When thou gatherest the grapes of thy vineyard, thou shalt not glean it afterward: it shall be for the *landborn*, for the fatherless, and for the widow.

22. And thou shalt remember that thou wast a bond-man in the land of Egypt; therefore I command thee to do this thing (Deut. xxiv).

22. And when ye reap the harvest of your land, thou shalt not make clean riddance of the corners of thy field when thou reapest, neither shalt thou gather any gleaning of thy harvest; thou shalt leave them unto the poor, and to the *landborn:* I am the Lord your God (Lev. xxiii).

28. At the end of three years thou shalt bring forth all the tithe of thine increase the same year, and shalt lay it up within thy gates:

29. And the Levite (because he hath no part nor inheritance with thee) and the *landborn*, and the

ploughmen and your vinedressers.—Dr. Alexander's rendering of Isai. lxi, 5.]

..10. He that chastiseth the heathen, *nations* (*goyim* — *Ethn.*) shall not he correct? he that teacheth man knowledge, shall not he know? (Ps. xciv).

10. But the man would not tarry that night, but he rose up and departed, and came over against Jebus, which is Jerusalem; and there were with him two asses saddled, his concubine also was with him.

11. And when they were by Jebus, the day was far spent; and the servant said unto his master, Come, I pray thee, and let us turn in unto the city of the Jebusites, and lodge in it.

12. And his master said unto him, We will not turn aside hither into the city of a *stranger* (*nokr.—allotr.*) that is not of the children

fatherless, and the widow, which are within thy gates, shall come, and shall eat and be satisfied; that the Lord thy God may bless thee in all the work of thine hand which thou doest (Deut. xiv).

12. When thou hast made an end of tithing all the tithes of thine increase the third year, which is the year of tithing, and hast given it unto the Levite, the *landborn*, the fatherless, and the widow, that they may eat within thy gates and be filled;

13. Then thou shalt say before the Lord thy God, I have brought away the hallowed things out of mine house, and also have given them unto the Levite, and unto the *landborn*, to the fatherless, and to the widow, according to all thy commandments, which thou hast commanded me; I have not transgressed thy commandments, neither have I forgotten them;

14. I have not eaten thereof in my mourning, neither have I taken away aught thereof for any unclean use, nor given aught thereof for the dead: but I have hearkened to the voice of the Lord my God, and have done according to all that thou hast commanded me.

15. Look down from thy holy habitation, from heaven, and bless thy people Israel, and the land which thou hast given us, as thou swarest unto our fathers, a land that floweth with milk and honey (Deut. xxvi).

19. Cursed is he that perverteth the judgment of the *landborn*, fatherless, and widow. And all the people shall say, Amen (Deut. xxvii).

10. Ye stand this day all of you before the Lord your God; your captains of your tribes, your elders, and your officers, with all the men of Israel.

11. Your little ones, your wives, and thy *landborn* that is in thy camp, from the hewer of thy wood unto the drawer of thy water:

12. That thou shouldest enter into covenant with the Lord thy God, and into his oath, which the Lord thy God maketh with thee this day:

13. That he may establish thee to-day for a people unto himself, and that he may be unto thee a God, as he hath said unto thee, and as he hath sworn unto thy fathers, to Abraham, to Isaac, and to Jacob...

12. Gather the people together, men, and women, and children, and thy *landborn*, that is within thy

The Middle Wall of Partition.

of Israel, we will pass over to Gibeah.

13. And he said unto his servant, Come, and let us draw near to one of these places to lodge all night, in Gibeah, or in Ramah (Judges xix).

4. And David and all Israel went to Jerusalem, which is Jebus; where the Jebusites were, the inhabitants of the land.

5. And the inhabitants of Jebus said to David, Thou shalt not come hither. Nevertheless David took the castle of Zion, which is the city of David.

6. And David said, Whosoever smiteth the Jebusites first shall be chief and captain. So Joab the son of Zeruiah went first up, and was chief (1 Chron. xi).

..16. For ye know how we have dwelt in the land of Egypt; and how we came through

SECTION III.—LANDBORN—LANDBORN BORN AGAIN.

thy gates, that they may hear, and that they may learn, and fear the Lord your God, and observe to do all the words of this law:

13. And that their children which have not known anything, may hear, and learn to fear the Lord your God, as long as ye live in the land whither ye go over Jordan to possess it................

7. Which executeth judgment for the oppressed; which giveth food to the hungry. The Lord looseth the prisoners.

8. The Lord openeth the eyes of the blind; the Lord raiseth them that are bowed down; the Lord loveth the righteous.

9. The Lord preserveth the *landborns*, he relieveth the fatherless and widow; but the way of the wicked he turneth upside down (Ps. cxlvi).

4. Trust ye not in lying words, saying, The temple of the Lord are these.

5. For if ye thoroughly amend your ways and your doings; if ye thoroughly execute judgment between a man and his neighbor;

6. If ye oppress not the *landborn*, the fatherless, and the widow, and shed not innocent blood in this place, neither walk after other gods to your hurt:

7. Then will I cause you to dwell in this place, in the land that I gave to your fathers, for ever and ever (Jer. vii).

3. Thus saith the Lord, Execute ye judgment and righteousness, and deliver the spoiled out of the hand of the oppressor; and do no wrong, do no violence to the *landborn*, the fatherless, nor the widow, neither shed innocent blood in this place (Jer. xxii).

7. In thee have they set light by father and mother; in the midst of thee have they dealt by oppression with the *landborn*; in thee have they vexed the fatherless and the widow.

29. The people of the land have used oppression, and exercised robbery, and have vexed the poor and needy; yea, they have oppressed the *landborn* wrongfully (Ezek. xxii).

8. And the word of the Lord came unto Zechariah, saying,

9. Thus speaketh the Lord of hosts, saying, Execute true judgment, and show mercy and compassion every man to his brother;

10. And oppress not the widow, nor the fatherless, the *landborn*, nor the poor; and let none of you imagine evil against his brother in your heart (Zech. vii).

The Mind of Will or Partition.

the *nations* which ye passed by (Deut. xxix).

..16. And the Lord said unto Moses, Behold, thou shalt sleep with thy fathers; and this people will rise up, and go a whoring after the gods of the *strangers* (*nokr.—allotr.*) of the land whither they go to be among them, and will forsake me, and break my covenant which I have made with them (Deut. xxxi).

5. And I will come near to you to judgment; and I will be a swift witness against the sorcerers, and against the adulterers, and against false swearers, and against those that oppress the hireling in his wages, the widow, and the fatherless, and that turn aside the *landborn* from his right, and fear not me, saith the Lord of hosts (Malachi iii).

[The original of the word rendered landborn, referred to in the above section, is in Hebrew *ger*, and the Greek rendering of the Hebrew word *ger* is *proselutos* in every instance, and while it is not always said to be the "proselutos in the gates," it is very evident that it is this class of persons so designated throughout. The language is uniform. They are associated with the Levite, who like themselves had no inheritance, also with the fatherless and widow. There is not a single instance, where language of a similar import is used respecting the *ger hgar*. The *ger* had no inheritance (Deut. xiv, 24);

21. So shall ye divide this land unto you according to the tribes of Israel.

22. And it shall come to pass, that ye shall divide it by lot for an inheritance unto you, and to the *landborns who are born again* (professedly, of course, and have made that profession in due form) among you which shall beget children among you; and they shall be unto you as the *Hebrew of the Hebrews* among the children of Israel; they shall have inheritance with you among the tribes of Israel.

23. And it shall come to pass, that in what tribe the *landborn is born again*, there shall ye give him his inheritance, saith the Lord

the *ger hgar* had an inheritance (Ez. xlvii, 23). The former were *dependent*, the latter were *independent*; hence this chapter of warnings, that he should not be oppressed in his dependent circumstances; and, up to the hour of his making a declaration of his faith —his new birth—it is enjoined in respect to him: When a "ger will act the ger"—is about to make a profession— thou shalt not *vex* him (Lev. xix, 33); but after he is circumcised and draws near and keeps the passover, he is called thenceforth *ger hgar*—is under the same law as the Hebrew of the Hebrews (Ex. xii, 49), and *thou shalt love him as thyself* (Lev. xix, 34). It is never said, *thou*

3. An Ammonite or Moabite shall not enter into the congregation of the Lord; even to their tenth generation shall they not enter into the congregation of the Lord for ever;

4. Because they met you not with bread and with water in the way, when ye came forth out of Egypt; and because they hired against thee Balaam the son of Beor, of Pethor of Mesopotamia, to curse thee.

5. Nevertheless the Lord thy God would not hearken unto Balaam; but the Lord thy God turned the curse into a blessing unto thee, because the Lord thy God loved thee.

6. Thou shalt not seek their peace nor their prosperity all thy days for ever [Deut. xxiii).

[The Ammonite and Moabite were to be treated or held as *sons of outland* or *peoples of the lands*, on account of their sin, till their tenth generation.]

"Not seek their peace nor prosperity all

SECTION III.—LANDBORN—LANDBORN BORN AGAIN.

	The line between Clean and Unclean.		*The Middle Wall of Partition.*	
God (Ezek. xlvii. See in full, page 51).	*shall love the ger* or *ger in the gates as thyself.*]		thy days forever" (Deut. xxiii, 6).	
This class received an inheritance. "The children of promise were counted for the seed"—"if children then heirs."	This class *had* no inheritance (Deut. xiv, 29) —might *buy* permanent possessions in the gates, unless redeemed within a year (Lev. xxv, 30).		"Nor seek their peace (*peoples of the lands*) or wealth for ever" (Ezra ix, 11, 12).	
They, of this class, who *ate* that which dieth of itself became unclean thereby (Lev. xvii, 15).	To this class they may *give* that which dieth of itself and he *may eat* it (Deut. xiv, 21).		To this class might *sell* that which dieth of itself (Deut. xiv, 21).	
These receiving an inheritance (Ez. xlvii, 22), of course gave *tithes*, and in their fields *gleaners* might come.	These *received tithes* (Deut. xiv, 21; xxvi, 12–15). *Gleaned* (Deut. xxiv, 19; Lev. xxiii, 22. See above.)		To these they must *give* neither *tithes* nor *wives*.	
The landborn born again *thou shalt love as thyself* (Lev. xix, 34).	Thou *shalt not hate* "thy brother" in thy heart (Lev. xix, 17).			
Thou shalt love "thy neighbor" *as thyself* (Lev. xix, 18).	Take thou no usury of "thy brother"—a *ger* and *toshabh*—a resident landborn or "proselyte of habitation" (Lev. xxv, 35–37).			
Of "his neighbor," the creditor shall not *exact* that lent in the year of release (Deut. xv, 2).	Of "his brother" the creditor shall not *exact* that lent in the year of release (Deut. xv, 2, 3).		Of a *nokri* you may *exact that lent* in the year of release (Deut. xv, 3).	
Not be an usurer to any of "my people poor by thee" (Ex. xxii, 25).	Not lend upon usury to "thy brother," usury of money, usury of victuals, etc. (Deut. xxiii, 19).		Unto a *nokri* thou mayest lend upon usury (Deut. xxiii, 20).	
[For the relations of these three classes, in reference to the passover, see page 50. Traced *logically* in small capitals.]	Ye exact usury a man of his "brother" (Neh. v, 7).		Thou mayest not set [a *nokri* king over thee, since he is not thy brother, Deut. xvii, 15].	

SECTION IV.—HEBREW, AND HEBREW OF THE HEBREWS.

"Stock of Israel"—*Consisting of* "*a Hebrew Man,*" ("*Thy Brother*" *whom* "*Thou shalt not hate*") *and a* "*Hebrew of the Hebrews,*" ("*Thy Neighbor*" *whom* "*Thou shalt love as thyself*").

42. Ye shall dwell in booths seven days; *every Hebrew of the Hebrews* (not "homeborn," as rendered) *in Israel* shall dwell in booths .. 22. And it shall come to pass, that ye shall divide it by lot for an inheritance unto you, and to the ger who act the ger (plural) among you, which shall beget children among you; and they shall be unto you *as the Hebrew of the Hebrews* (not "homeborn") *among the children of Israel;* they shall have inheritance with you among the tribes of Israel. 23. And it shall come to pass, in what tribe *a ger acts the ger*, there shall ye give him an inheritance, saith the Lord God (Ez. xlvii. See pages 51, 66). [29. The *Hebrew of the Hebrews* (not "homeborn") *among the children of Israel*, and to the landborn born again (ger acting	The line between Clean and Unclean.	...43. That *your generations* (your nation) may know that I made the children of Israel to dwell in booths, when I brought them out of the land of Egypt: I am the Lord your God (Lev. xxiii).

The Middle Wall of Partition.

SECTION IV.—HEBREW—HEBREW OF THE HEBREWS. 69

the ger) in your midst, one law (*torah*—requirement) shall be to you (both) in offering for a sin of ignorance.]

30. But the soul that doeth aught presumptuously, *of the Hebrew of the Hebrews, or of the landborn* (born again), the same reproacheth the Lord; and that soul shall *be cut off from among his people*..........

31. Because he hath despised the word of the Lord, and hath broken his commandments, that soul shall be *utterly cut off: his iniquity shall be upon him* (Num. xv)............

....

..thou shalt not vex him.

34. Like as the *azurah* of you (not "homeborn" of you)—as *the Hebrew of the Hebrews of you*—shall be among you so (shall be) the ger that acts the ger (*proselutos, prosporeuomenos*, Sept.) with you, and thou shalt love him as thyself..................

The line between Clean and Unclean.

..held as....................

....

[33. And if a (*ger yagur*—ger will act the ger, Heb.—*proselutos proselthea*, Sept.) landborn shall be born again with you, in your land ....

....

...for ye were *gerim—proselutoi*—landborns in the land of Egypt, Lev. xix.]

The Middle Wall of Partition.

..."a heathen man" or foreigner among his people — *excommunicated*.

..."The Lord hath *utterly separated* me (son of outland) from his people" (Isai. lvi, 3).

"Visiting the *iniquity* of the fathers upon the children unto the third and fourth generation of *them that hate me:*"— All emigrants of image-worshiping nations, or sons of outland, were "heathen men"—of the nations. (Except the third generation of an emigrant family of Egypt or Edom). To be held as such was to be left as the nations were left, to the uncovenanted mercy of God—not to be restored again to the Church.

...18. But thou shalt love "thy neighbor" as thyself (Lev. xix).	17. Thou shalt not hate "thy brother".. 12. And if *thy brother*, a *Hebrew man*, or a *Hebrew woman*, be sold unto thee, and serve thee six years (Deut. xv). 2. If thou buy an *Hebrew* servant, six years he shall serve; and in the seventh he shall go out free for nothing (Ex. xxi) 9. That every man should let his man-servant, and every man his maid servant, being a *Hebrew or a Hebrewess*, go free . . . to-wit, of a *Jew his brother*. 14. At the end of seven years let ye go every man *his brother a Hebrew*—(Jer. xxxiv).	

(Left margin: *Clean and Unclean.* Right margin: *The Middle Wall of Partition.*)

SECTION V.—CIRCUMCISION—UNCIRCUMCISION.

The Circumcised, Uncircumcised, and Uncircumcision.

9. And the Lord spake unto Moses, saying, 10. Speak unto the children of Israel, saying, If any man of you or of your posterity shall be unclean by reason of a dead body, or be in a journey afar off, yet he shall keep the passover unto the Lord.	1. And the apostles and brethren that were in Judea, heard that the *Gentiles* (*Ethn.—nations*) had also received the word of God. 3. Saying, Thou wentest in to men uncircumcised (the uncircumcision) *and didst eat with them* (Acts xi). 11. But now I have

SECTION V.—CIRCUMCISION—UNCIRCUMCISION. 71

11. The fourteenth day of the second month at even they shall keep it, and eat it with unleavened bread and bitter herbs.

12. They shall leave none of it unto the morning, nor break any bone of it: according to all the ordinances of the passover they shall keep it.

13. But the man that is clean and is not in a journey and forbeareth to keep the passover, even the same soul shall *be cut off from among his people*.................. because he brought not the offering of the Lord in his appointed season ....

.... and keep the passover unto the Lord; according to *the ordinance of the passover* (see Ex. xii, 43–49); and according to the manner thereof, so shall he do [ye shall have one ordinance for the *ger* and for the *azurah* of the land]. (Num. ix),

(See page 48, how the *ger* came to be classed with the *azurah*).

19. Seven days shall there be no leaven found in your houses; for

The line between Clean and Unclean.

.. [treated as a...........

....

14. And if a stranger shall sojourn (*ger yagur*, Heb.—*proselutos proselthea*, Sept.)—a landborn shall be born again among you................

....

The Middle Wall of Partition.

written unto you *not to keep company;* if any man that is called a brother be a fornicator, or covetous, or an idolater, or a railer, or a drunkard, or an extortioner; with such a one no *not to eat* (1 Cor. v).

17. And if he shall neglect to hear them, tell it unto the church: but if he neglect to hear the church, let him be unto thee as a *heathen man—Ethnikos—as one of the nations* (Matt. xviii).

.. *nokri* — foreigner or " heathen man."]

.. that man shall *bear his sin*—once a foreigner, always a foreigner.

14 And if any man obey not our word by this epistle, note that man, and have *no company with him*, that he may be ashamed.

15. Yet count him not as an enemy, but admonish him as a brother (2 Thess. iii).

9. I wrote unto you in an epistle *not to company* with fornicators;

10. Yet not altogether with the fornicators of this world, or with the covetous, or extortioners, or with idolaters; for then must ye needs go out of the world (1 Cor. v).

whosoever eateth that which is leavened, even that soul shall be *cut off from the congregation of Israel* .... (who ate the passover, Ex. xii, 47) whether he be of the landborn (born again) or of the Hebrew of the Hebrews, Ex. xii. Compare with previous verse.

5. That I may take the house of Israel in their own heart, because they are estranged from me through their idols.

7. For every one of the house of Israel and of the ger which will act the ger in Israel (*ger asher yayur*, Heb.— proselutoon proseluteuontoon — "proselytes," "proselyted" or landborus," proselyted" Sept.) which separateth himself from me, and setteth up his idols in his heart and putteth the stumbling-block of his iniquity before his face, and cometh to a prophet to inquire of him concerning me; I the Lord will answer him by myself:

8. And I will set my face against that man, and will make him a sign and a proverb, and I will cut him off from the midst of my people; and ye shall know that I am the Lord (Ezek. xiv).

....

.. entered into *her sanctuary*, whom thou didst

.. [treated as a *proselutos*—landborn, or one of *the people of the land*— . as the unclean.]

....

The Line between Clean and Unclean.

[The Jews had "no *dealings*" or *associations* with the Samaritans. They might lend to the *nokri* upon usury, and exact that lent in the year of release (Deut. xv, 3 ; xxiii, 20); hence such "dealings" were proper, but no "associations"—such *as eating*, etc.]

15. And one of them, when he saw that he was healed, turned back, and with a loud voice glorified God:

16. And fell down on his face at his feet, giving him thanks; and he was a Samaritan.

17. And Jesus answering said, Were there not ten cleansed? but where are the nine?

18. There are not found that returned to give glory to God, save this stranger—*allogenes* (Luke xvii).

Any *allogenes* shall not eat of it (the passover, Ex. xii, 43, Sept.).

10. The adversary hath spread out his hand upon all her pleasant things; for she hath seen that the heathen (*goyim*, Heb — *Ethn.*, Sept.)—*nations*. .

....

The Middle Wall of Partition.

SECTION V.—CIRCUMCISION—UNCIRCUMCISION. 73

command that they should not enter into *thy congregation* (*khahal*, Heb.—*ecclesia*, Sept.)—Church (Lam. i).

5. And the Lord said unto me, Son of man .. mark well the entering in of the house, with every going forth of *the sanctuary*.

6. And thou shalt say ... O ye house of Israel, let it suffice you of all your abominations.

7. In that ye have brought *into my sanctuary*..................

....

...to be in *my sanctuary*, to pollute it, even my house, when ye offer my bread, the fat and the blood, and they have broken my covenant because of all your abominations.

8. And ye have not kept the charge of my holy things; but ye have set keepers of my charge in *my sanctuary* for yourselves.

9. Thus saith the Lord God...............

The Line between Clean and Unclean.

....

....

The Middle Wall of Partition.

.. strangers (*benei nekar*)—sons of outland—uncircumcised in heart, and uncircumcised in flesh..................

....

[Any son of outland; the uncircumcised in heart and uncircumcis-ed in flesh,[*] belong-

---

[*] A *landborn* but not a *ger—proselutos* in thy gates—not having disowned kindred and friends; not having foresworn his nationality; still having "dealings" or associations with foreigners. The child of an emigrant family born in the Holy Land, while he remained connected with his father's family (a family of outlands), was held as one of them—was not a *ger—proselutos*. Hence,

74 CHART.

	Clean and Unclean.		Wall of Partition.	
... *my sanctuary* (Ez. xliv).				ing to any son of outland.] which is among the children of Israel shall not enter............
1. For the Lord will have mercy on Jacob, and will yet choose Israel, and set them in their own land; and the..........................		.. *strangers — gerim — landborns*...............		
..shall be joined with them, and they shall cleave to the house of Jacob (Isai. xiv).				
23. Ye shall not walk in the manners of............				..the *nations* which I cast out before you... (Lev. xx).
24. But I have said unto you, ye shall inherit their land, and I will give it unto you to possess it, a land that floweth with milk and honey; I am the Lord your God, which have separated you from......				..the *peoples* (Sept., na-tions).
26. And ye shall be holy unto me; for I the Lord am holy, and have severed you from.............				..the *peoples* (Sept., na-tions, Lev. xx).
2. For thou art an holy people unto the Lord thy God, and the Lord hath chosen thee to be a peculiar people unto himself, above all........................			The Middle	..[*the peoples* which are upon the face of the ground—*adamah*] (Deu. xiv).
13. Now, therefore, I pray thee, if I have found grace in thy sight, show me now thy way, that I may know thee, that I may find grace in thy sight; and consider that *this nation* (*goy.*, Heb.—*Ethn.*, Sept.) is thy people.				1. By the rivers of Babylon there we sat down; yea, we wept, when we remembered Zion.
14. And he said, My presence shall go with thee, and I will give thee rest.				
15. And he said unto him, If thy presence go not with me, carry us not up hence.				4. How shall we sing the Lord's song [upon
16. For wherein shall it be known here that I and				(*nekar—allotr.*) foreign

those " belonging to any son of outland shall not enter my sanctuary." Following the usual renderings of Hebrew into Greek, by the LXX, I would render the Greek as follows:—Thus saith the Lord God: Any (landborn) son of a son of outland, among all the (landborn) sons of the sons of outland who are in the midst of the house of Israel, uncircumcised in heart and uncircumcised in flesh, shall not enter my sanctuary.

SECTION V.— CIRCUMCISION—UNCIRCUMCISION. 75

thy people have found grace in thy sight? Is it not in that thou goest with us? So shalt we be separated, I and thy people,..

11. But when Peter was come to Antioch, I withstood him to the face, because he was to be blamed.

12. For before that certain came from James, he did eat ....

....

......come, he withdrew and separated himself, fearing them which were of *the circumcision* (Gal. ii).

16. Then Paul stood up, and beckoning with his hand, said, Men of Israel, and.................................

50. But the Jews stirred up the........................

19. Now they which were scattered abroad upon the persecution that arose about Stephen, traveled as far as Phenice, and Cyprus, and Antioch, preaching the word to none but unto the *Jews only* (Acts xi).

34. Then Peter opened his mouth, and said, Of a truth I perceive that God is no respecter of persons :..

2. And when Peter was come up to Jerusalem, they that were of *the circumcision* contended with him ....

The Apostle was in favor of

ground or soil —*adamah*] (Ps.cxxxvii).

..[from *every people* which are upon the face of the ground—*adamah*] (Ex. xxxiii).

..., with the Gentiles (*Ethn.* — *nations*), but when they were...........

....

..ye *that fear* God (pious "Gentiles") give audience (Acts xiii).

.. *devout and honorable women* (not "proselytes"), and the chief men of the city, and raised persecution against Paul and Barnabas, and expelled them out of their coasts (Acts xiii).

... Cornelius, a centurion of the band called the Italian band,

2. A devout man, and one that *feared God* (not a "proselyte") with all his house, which gave much alms to the people, and prayed to God always.

..35. But in every *nation* (*Ethn.*) he that feareth him, and worketh righteousness ("the outcasts of Israel" "will I gather"—pious "Gentiles," Isai. lvi, 8) is accepted with him (Acts x).

..3. Saying, Thou wentest in to men *uncircumcised* (*the uncircumcision*), and didst eat with them (Acts xi).

SECTION VI.—SACRIFICES AND OFFERINGS.

The Positions in the previous Sections, as Confirmed and Illustrated in the Law of Sacrifices and Offerings, and in Tradition.

[13. Every Hebrew of the Hebrews (*azurah*) shall do these things after this manner, in offering an offering made by fire of a sweet savour unto the Lord ..

...... as ye (Hebrew of the Hebrews, and landborn born again) do ..

15. The congregation (*khahal*—Church), the same ordinance (*hokh*—" manner " of observance) shall be for both you and the landborn born again (*ger hgar*, Heb. — *proselutos proskei*, Sept.); an ordinance (*hokh*—" manner " of observance) forever .

....
...... as ye (the Church) so ....

..14. And if a stranger shall sojourn (*ger yagur*, Heb.—*proselutos, prosgenetai*, Sept.) — landborn shall be born again — or whosoever shall be in your midst belonging to *your generations* (*geneas*, Sept., rendered *nation*, Phil. ii. 15), and will offer an offering made by fire, of a sweet savour unto the Lord : ....
....

...... so he (whosoever is of your nation) shall do.

...... for *your generations* (your nation) :............
....

...... shall the landborn (*ger* — *proselutos*) be before the face of the

[" Josephus says : there was in the court of the temple a wall, or balustrade, breast high, with pillars at particular distances, and inscriptions on them in Greek and Latin, importing that strangers (foreigners) were forbidden from entering further; here their offerings were received, and sacrifices were offered for them, they standing at the barrier; but were not allowed to approach the altar.

From the above particulars we learn the meaning of what the Apostle calls " the Middle Wall of Partition " between Jews and Gentiles broken down by the gospel."—*Watson*.

In the light of the above, the following allusions are manifest : " Neither let the son of outland who hath joined himself (pious "Gentiles ") to the Lord speak, saying, The Lord hath utterly separated me from his people," for " their burnt-offerings and their sacrifices shall be accepted upon mine altar; for mine house shall be called a house

SECTION VI.—SACRIFICES AND OFFERINGS

......16. One law (*torah*—requirement) and one judgment (penalty) shall be for you and for the landborn born again (*ger hgar — proselutos proskei.*) among you, Num. xv.]

17. And the Lord spake unto Moses, saying,

18. Speak unto Aaron, and to his sons, and unto all the children of Israel, and say unto them, Whatsoever he be of the house of Israel............

8. And thou shalt say unto them, Whatsoever man there be of the house of Israel, or of the ger which will act the ger among you (Heb. *ger asher yagur*— Sept. *proselutoon proskeimenoon* — landborns " added" or "attached" to you) that offereth a burnt-offering or sacrifice.

9. And bringeth it not unto the door of the tabernacle of the congregation, to offer it unto the Lord; even that man shall be *cut off from among his people* ("people of the congregation" at least) (Lev. xvii).

Lord ....
....

[" One requirement " and " one manner " of requirement for the Church (composed of the Hebrew of the Hebrews and landborn born again), and "one manner of observance " for the whole nation; but *not* "one manner of observance" for Jews and Gentiles "before the face of the Lord "— at the altar. The Gentiles (nations) were never permitted to enter that "court," in which was the altar, where the Jews as a nation offered sacrifice.]

......or of the stranger (*ger*— *proselutos*)—landborn—in Israel, that will offer his oblation for all his vows, and for all his free-will-offerings, which they will offer unto the Lord for a burnt-offering;

19. Ye shall offer at your own will a male without blemish, of the beeves, of the sheep, or of the goats............

[The presentation of an offering within the court of the Jewish nation, was not the peculiar prerogative of any class of persons of the Jewish nation. Sacrifices were required of persons guilty of an offense against the church before restoration to a

of prayer for all *peoples*" (Sept., *nations*) Isai. lvi, 3, 7.]

[The prophet, in the above, alludes to the privileges of "Gentiles" or foreigners in the place appointed them in the Temple, to-wit: "The court of the Gentiles." See Solomon's Prayer, 2 Kings viii, 41, page 55; also 2 Chron. vi, 32, page 5.]

......25. Neither from a stranger's hand (*ben nekar*)--from the hand of a son of outland—shall ye offer the bread of your God of any of these; because their corruption is in them, and blemishes be in them; they shall not be accepted for you (Lev. xxii).

[Vertical text between columns: The Living Wall of Partition — Middle Wall of Partition — Clean and Unclean]

13. And if the *whole congregation of Israel* (who ate the passover, Ex. xii, 47) sin through ignorance, and the thing be hid from the eyes of the *assembly* (*khahal* — Church) and they have done somewhat against any of the commandments of the Lord, concerning things which should not be done, and are guilty, etc. (Lev. iv).

[Unclean] place among the clean; also of the landborn upon entering the Church. Among things required of a "complete proselyte"—"proselyte of righteousness" or landborn born again, was "circumcision and sacrifice"—*Tradition.*]

[Clean] There being one ordinance (*hokh*—manner of observance) to the whole *nation*, as referred to above, the inspired writers often do not refer to any distinction between *the Clean and the Unclean*, but use terms that apply to the *whole nation*. Hence in the following, it is *the Prince*—civil ruler—and *the people of the land*—all citizens of the commonwealth or the Jewish nation. See above, Section II.]

22. And if ye have erred, and not observed all these commandments which the Lord hath spoken unto Moses,

23. Even all that the Lord hath commanded you by the hand of Moses, from the day that the Lord commanded Moses, and henceforward among your *generations* (Sept. *geneas* — your *nation* — "in the midst of a crooked and perverse *nation*," *geneas*, Phil. ii, 15.) (Num. xv.)

[A Moabite of the tenth, an Edomite of the third generation (*geneas*) "in thy gates," were *your generations*—were of *your nation*.]

22. So that the *generation to come* (your nation in after-times) of your *children* (all were *children* who were not *allotrioi* — *foreigners*, see Matt. xvii, 25, 26, page 46; and all were *brothers* who were not *nokrim*—foreigners, Deut. xv, 2, 3, page 45) shall rise up after you and.............. ....

[The Middle Wall of Partition]

[Those ministering at the altar, inside "this barrier" or wall, where the altar stood, "received" over this wall "at the hands of a son of outland," "standing outside this barrier," his "burnt-offerings and sacrifices," and they were "offered for him" upon the altar.]

......the stranger (*nokr — allotr.*) that shall come from a far land, shall say, when they see the plagues of that land, and the sicknesses which the Lord hath laid upon it:

23. And that the

22. When a ruler (*nasi*, Heb.) hath sinned, and done somewhat through ignorance against any of the commandments of the Lord his God, concerning things which should not be done, and is guilty;

23. Or if his sin, wherein he hath sinned, come to his knowledge; he shall bring his offering, a kid of the goats, a male without blemish;

SECTION VI.—SACRIFICES AND OFFERINGS.

27. [And if any soul of *the people of the land*] sin through ignorance, while he doeth somewhat against any of the commandments of the Lord, concerning things which ought not to be done, and be guilty;

28. Or, if his sin which he hath sinned, come to his knowledge; then he shall bring his offering, a kid of the goats, a female without blemish, for his sin which he hath sinned.

29. And he shall lay his hand upon the head of the sin-offering, and slay the sin-offering in the place of the burnt-offering.

30. And the priest shall take of the blood thereof with his finger, and put it upon the horns of the altar of burnt-offering, and shall pour out all the blood thereof at the bottom of the altar (Lev. iv).

27. And if any soul (of the people of the land) sin through ignorance, then he shall bring a she-goat of the first year for a sin-offering.

28. And the priest shall make an atonement for the soul that sinneth ignorantly, when he sinneth by ignorance before the Lord, to make an atonement for him; and it shall be forgiven him (Num. xv).

7. And a portion shall be for the prince (*nasi*, Heb.) on the one side and on the other side of the oblation of the holy portion, and of the possessions of the city, before the oblation of the holy portion, and before the possession of the city, from the west side westward, and from the east side eastward; and the length shall be over against one of the portions, from the west border unto the east border.

8. In the land shall be his possession in Israel; and my princes (*nasiai*, Heb.—plural) shall no more oppress my people; and the rest of *the land shall they give to the house of Israel according to their tribes*. (See Ez. xlvii, 22, 23, and pages 66, 67.)

9. Thus saith the Lord God, Let it suffice you, O princes (*nasiai*) of Israel; remove violence and spoil, and execute judgment and justice, take away your exactions from my people, saith the Lord God.

16. All the *people of the land* shall give this oblation for the prince (*nasi*) in Israel.

17. And it shall be the prince's (*nasi*) part to give burnt-offerings, and meat-offerings, and drink-offer-

whole land thereof is brimstone, and salt, and burning, that it is not sown, nor beareth, nor any grass groweth therein, like the overthrow of Sodom, and Gomorrah, Admah, and Zeboim, which the Lord overthrew in his anger, and in his wrath;

24. Even all *nations* (*goyim — Ethn.*) shall say, Wherefore hath the Lord done thus unto this land? what meaneth the heat of this great anger?

25. Then men shall say, Because they have forsaken the covenant of the Lord God of their fathers, which he made with them when he brought them forth out of the land of Egypt (Deut. xxix).

3. Incline your ear, and come unto me: hear, and your soul shall live; and I will make an everlasting covenant *with you* (with every one that thirsteth) even the sure mercies of David.

4. Behold, I have given him for a witness to the *peoples*, a leader and commander to the *peoples* (the latter *nations*, Sept.) (Isai. lv).

10. And in that day there shall be a root of Jesse, which shall stand for an ensign of the *peoples*, to it shall the *nations* seek; and his

ings, in the feasts, and in the new moons, and in the sabbaths, in all solemnities of the house of Israel; he shall prepare the sin-offering, and the meat-offering, and the burnt-offering, and the peace-offerings, to make reconciliation for the house of Israel.

22. And upon that day shall the prince (*nasi*) prepare for himself, and for all the *people of the land*, a bullock for a sin-offering.

[22. And upon that day shall the *prince* prepare for himself and *his house*, and for all the *people of the land*, etc., Sept.]

23. And seven days of the feast he shall prepare a burnt-offering to the Lord, seven bullocks and seven rams without blemish, daily the seven days; and a kid of the goats daily for a sin-offering (Ezek. xlv).

2. And the prince (*nasi*) shall enter by the way of the porch of that gate without, and shall stand by the post of the gate, and the priest shall prepare his burnt-offering and his peace-offerings, and he shall worship at the threshold of the gate; then he shall go forth; but the gate shall not be shut until the evening.

3. Likewise the *people of the land* shall worship at the door of the gate before the Lord, in the sabbaths, and in the new moons.

4. And the burnt-offering that the prince (*nasi*) shall offer unto the Lord in the sabbath-day shall be six lambs without blemish, and a ram without blemish.

8. And when the prince (*nasi*) shall enter, he shall go in by the way of the porch of that gate, and he shall go forth by the way thereof.

9. But when the *people of the land* shall come before the Lord in the solemn feasts, he that entereth in by the way of the north gate to worship shall go out by the way of the south gate, and he that entereth by the way of the south gate shall go forth by the way of the north gate; he shall not return by the way of the gate whereby he came in, but shall go forth over against it.

10. And the prince (*nasi*) in the midst of them, when they go in, shall go in; and when they go forth, shall go forth:

rest shall be glorious.

12. And he shall set up an ensign for the *nations*, and shall assemble the *outcasts of Israel*, and gather together the dispersed of Judah from the four corners of the earth (Isai. xi).

29. Lord, now lettest thou thy servant depart in peace according to thy word;

30. For mine eyes have seen thy salvation.

31. Which thou hast prepared before the face of all *peoples*.

32. A light to lighten the *nations*, and the glory of thy people Israel (Luke ii).

25. Who by the mouth of thy servant David hast said, Why did the *nations* (*Ethn.*) rage, and the *peoples* imagine vain things? (Acts iv.)

8. Now I say that Jesus Christ was a minister of the circumcision for the truth of God, to confirm the promises made unto the fathers;

9. And that the *nations* might glorify God for his mercy; as it is written, For this cause I will confess to be among the *nations*, and sing unto thy name.

10. And again he saith, Rejoice, ye *nations*, with his people.

11. And again, Praise the Lord, all ye *nations*;

SECTION VI.—SACRIFICES AND OFFERINGS. 81

16. Thus saith the Lord God, if the prince (*nasi*) give a gift unto any of his sons, the inheritance thereof shall be his sons'; it shall be their possession by inheritance.

17. But if he give a gift of his inheritance to one of his servants, then it shall be his to the year of liberty; after it shall return to the prince (*nasi*); but his inheritance shall be his sons' for them.

18. Moreover, the prince (*nasi*) shall not take of the people's inheritance by oppression, to thrust them out of their possession; but he shall give his sons' inheritance out of his own possession; *that my people be not scattered every man from his possession* (Ezekiel xlvi).

11. And Urijah the priest built an altar according to all that king Ahaz had sent from Damascus; so Urijah the priest made it against king Ahaz came from Damascus.

15. And king Ahaz commanded Urijah the priest, saying, Upon the great altar burn the morning burnt-offering, and the evening meat-offering, and the king's burnt-sacrifice, and his meat-offerings, with the burnt-offering of all the *people of the land*, and their meat-offering ... and the brazen altar shall be for me to inquire by (2 Kings xvi).

9. And God said unto Abraham, thou shalt keep my covenant, therefore, thou, and thy seed after thee, *in their generations* (*geneas*—in your nation). (Gen. xvii.)

The Middle Wall of Partition.

and laud him, all ye peoples.

12. And again, Esaias saith, There shall be a root of Jesse, and he that shall rise to reign over the *nations*, in him shall the *nations* trust (Rom. xv).

10. Then she fell on her face, and bowed herself to the ground, and said unto him, Why have I found grace in thine eyes, that thou shouldest take knowledge of me, seeing I am a stranger (*nokri—zenos*). (Ruth ii.)

19. Then said the king to Ittai the Gittite, Wherefore goest thou also with us? return to thy place, and abide with the king; for thou art a stranger (*nokri—zenos*), and also an exile (2 Sam. xv).

7. And they took counsel, and bought with them the potter's field to bury strangers (*zenoi*—pious "Gentiles") in (Matt. xxvii).

[Pious foreigners among the Jews, such as Ittai the Gittite, etc., in Greek, were called *zenoi*, or *zenoi* "from the covenants of promise" (Eph. ii, 12, 19), not being permitted a covenant relation or membership in the Jewish Church, under the covenant with Abraham.]

22. And they said, Cornelius the centurion, a just man, and one

......and of good report among all the *nation of the Jews*, was warned from God by a holy angel, to send for thee into his house and to hear words of thee.

28. And he said unto them, Ye know how that it is an unlawful thing for a man that is a *Jew* (of the Jewish nation) *to keep company*, or come..............

45. And they of the *circumcision* (*the Jewish nation*) which believed were astonished, as many as came with Peter, because that on........................

......by that which is called *the circumcision in the flesh made by hands* (the Jewish nation);..............

..........within the commonwealth of Israel (or among "the people of the land") and....................

The Middle Wall of Partition.

(one of the nations fearing God, or a pious "Gentile") that feareth God......................

..unto one of *another nation;* but God hath showed me that I should not call any man common or unclean.

..the *nations* (*the uncircumcision*) also were poured out the gift of the Holy Ghost (Acts x).

11. Wherefore remember, that ye being *in time past* (under the Jewish economy) Gentiles (*nations*) in the flesh who are called *uncircumcision*............

..12. That at that time (under that economy) ye were without Christ (without "the oracles of God") being aliens (*apo-allotrioomenoi*)— held as foreigners..........

...strangers (*xenoi*) from the covenants of promise, etc. (See exposition, Chap. III.)

19. Now therefore ye are no more strangers (*xenoi*, as Ittai, a pious foreigner) and foreigners (*paroikoi*—dwellers — resident foreigners, who may not eat the

SECTION VI.—SACRIFICES AND OFFERINGS. 83

...... fellow-citizens of the saints and of the household (one of the nations could not become a citizen within the Jewish nation, nor a member of a household of God, under the covenant with Abraham) of God (Eph. ii).

...... nigh (as the Jewish nation) by the blood of Christ.

Partition.

passover, Ex. xii, 43, Sept.); but......

13. But *now* in Christ Jesus ye who (in time past) were far off (the nations) are made......

14. For he is our peace, who hath made both one, AND HATH BROKEN DOWN THE MIDDLE WALL OF PARTITION BETWEEN US.

15. Having abolished in his flesh the enmity, even the law of commandments contained in ordinances; for to make in himself of twain one new man, so making peace;

16. And that he might reconcile both (the pious of both the Jewish *nation* and of other *nations*) unto God in one body by the cross, having slain the enmity thereby,

17. And came and preached peace to them that were afar off ("Gentiles"—nations) and to them that are nigh (Jewish nation).

18. For through him we both (circumcision and uncircumcision—those of the Jewish nation and those of other nations) have access by one Spirit unto the Father.

19. *Now* (under the new economy) ye are no more (as under the old economy) strangers—*xenoi* (pious foreigners or *nokri*, such as Ittai, etc., called, in relation to the covenants of promise, *xenoi*) and foreigners—*paroikoi*, dwellers, resident foreigners (called, in relation to the citizens of the Hebrew commonwealth or "the people of the land," dwellers or resident foreigners) but fellow-citizens (under this new economy) of the saints and of the household (under this new economy) of God.

20. And are built upon the foundation of the apostles and prophets, Jesus Christ himself being the chief corner-stone:

21. In whom all the building, fitly framed together, groweth unto a holy temple in the Lord.

22. In whom ye also are builded (*the nations* formed no part of *that building—the Church built* up under the covenant with Abraham) together for a habitation of God through the Spirit (Eph. ii).

1. For this cause I Paul, the prisoner of Jesus Christ for you Gentiles (*nations—the uncircumcision*, to whom Paul was minister), etc.

5. Which in other ages was not made known unto the sons of men, as it is now revealed unto his holy apostles and prophets by the Spirit;

6. That the Gentiles (*nations*) should be fellow-heirs, and of the same body, and partakers of his promise (the pious of the *nations*, hitherto, were "strangers from the covenants of *promise*") in Christ by the gospel (Eph. iii).

SECTION VII.—REMAINING REFERENCES.

Remaining References, and Extent of the Privileges of the Cities of Refuge.

29. And this shall be a statute for ever unto you, that in the seventh month, on the tenth day of the month, ye shall afflict your souls, and do no work at all, whether it be a **Hebrew of the Hebrews or landborn born again**-- (*ger hgar*, Heb.—*proselutos proskei.*, Sept.) among you.

33. And he shall make an atonement for the holy sanctuary, and he shall make an atonement for the tabernacle of the congregation, and for the altar; and he shall make an atonement for the priests, and for *all the people of the congregation* (*khahal*, Heb.—*ecclesia*, Sept.)—Church (Lev. xvi).

10. Whatsoever man there be of the house of Israel or of **the landborn born again** (*ger hgar*, Heb.—*pros. proskei*, Sept.) among you, that eateth any manner of blood, I will even set my face against that soul that eateth blood, and will cut him off from among his people.

12. Therefore I said unto the children of Israel, No soul of you

12. Six days thou shalt do thy work, and on the seventh day thou shalt rest; that thine ox and thine ass may rest, and the son of thy handmaid and **the landborn** (*ger*, Heb.—*pros.*, Sept.) may be refreshed (Ex. xxiii).

14. But the seventh day is the sabbath of the Lord thy God: in it thou shalt not do any work, thou, nor thy son, nor thy daughter, nor thy man-servant, nor thy maid-servant, nor thine ox, nor thine ass, nor any of thy cattle, nor **thy landborn** (*ger*, Heb.—*proselutos*, Sept.) that is within thy gates; that thy man-servant and thy maid-servant may rest as well as thou (Deu. v).

16. And I charged your judges at that time, saying, Hear the causes between your brethren, and judge righteously between every man and his brother, and **the landborn** (*ger—pros.*) that is with him (Deut. i).

43. **The landborn** (*ger—pros.*) *that is within thee* shall get up above thee very high;

["Thou wilt save me from the strifes of the people; thou wilt place me at the head (or for a chief) of *nations;* a people I have not known shall serve me. At the hearing of the ear they will obey me, the sons of outland will lie to me; the sons of outland will decay and tremble out of their inclosures."—Dr. J. Addison Alexander's rendering of Ps. xviii, 44-46.]

44. Thou also hast delivered me from the strivings of my people, thou hast kept me to be head of the *nations;* a people which I knew not shall serve me.

45. The sons of outland (*benei nekar*) shall submit themselves unto me: as soon as they hear, they shall be obedient unto me.

46. The sons of outland (*benei nekar*) shall fade away, and they shall be afraid out of their close places (2 Sam. xxii).

10. And the sons of outland (*benei nekar*) shall build up thy walls, and their kings shall minister unto thee: for

SECTION VII.—REMAINING REFERENCES. 85

shall eat blood, neither shall any **landborn born again** (*ger hgar*, Heb.— *pros proskei*, Sept.) among you eat blood.

13. And whatsoever man there be of the children of Israel, or of **the landborn born again** (*ger hgar—pros proskei*) which hunteth and catcheth any beast or fowl that may be eaten; he shall even pour out the blood thereof, and cover it with dust (Lev. xvii).

26. Ye shall therefore keep my statutes and my judgments, and shall not commit any of these abominations; neither any **Hebrew of the Hebrews or landborn born again** (*ger hgar — pros. prosgenomenos*) among you;

29. For whosoever shall commit any of these abominations, even the souls that commit them shall be cut off from among their people (Lev. xviii).

16. And he that blasphemeth the name of the Lord, he shall surely be put to death, and all the congregation (*gadath*—not the "*gadath* of Israel," who ate the passover, Ex. xii, 47) shall certainly stone him; as well the **landborn (born again) as the Hebrew of the Hebrews**), when he blasphemeth the name

and thou shalt come down very low.

44. He shall lend to thee, and thou shalt not lend to him; he shall be the head, and thou shalt be the tail (Deut. xxviii).

[The phrase italicised in Deut. xxviii, 43, above, is a peculiar phrase in the original. It should, perhaps, be rendered: *The landborn which is among thy drawing nigh;* that is, *the landborn in the Church,* or that element of *the Church* which is of "stock" not "of Israel," shall become chief and the disobedient Jews shall be rejected and "become an astonishment, a proverb and a byword among *all nations* whither the Lord shall lead thee."]

11. And thou shalt rejoice in every good thing which the Lord thy God hath given unto thee, and unto thy house, thou and the Levite, and **the landborn** (*ger — pros.*) that is among you (Deut. xxvi).

10. But the seventh day . . . nor thy **landborn** (*ger — pros.*) in thy gates (Ex. xx).

32. **The landborn** (Heb. *ger*—Sept. *xenos !*) did not lodge in the street; but I opened my doors to the traveler (Job xxxi).

[The above is the on-

in my wrath I smote thee, but in my favour have I had mercy on thee (Isai. lx).

15. Are we not counted of him **foreigners** (*nokr.—allotr.*) for he hath sold us, and hath quite devoured also our money (Gen. xxxi).

21. For the Lord shall rise up as in mount Perazim, he shall be wroth as in the valley of Gibeon, that he may do his work, his strange work; and bring to pass his act, his **foreign** (*nokr.— allotr.*) act (Isai. xxviii).

34. Quenched the violence of fire, escaped the edge of the sword, out of weakness were made strong, waxed valiant in fight, turned to fight the armies of the aliens (*allotr.*)—**foreigners** (Heb. xi).

21. Yet I had planted thee a noble vine, wholly a right seed; how then art thou turned into the degenerate plant of a **foreign** (*nokr.—allotr.*) vine unto me? (Jer. ii).

15. They that dwell in mine house, and my maids, count me for a stranger (*zar*, see Chap. V); I am a **foreigner** (*nokr.—allotr.*) in thy sight.

. . to sell her unto a strange nation (*nokr.*, **foreign people**, Heb.— *allotr.*, **foreign nation**, Sept.) he shall have no

of the Lord, shall be put to death.

22. Ye shall have one manner of law as well for **the landborn (born again) as for the Hebrew of the Hebrews**; for I am the Lord your God (Lev. xxiv).

32. And he wrote there upon the stones a copy of the law of Moses, which he wrote in the presence of the children of Israel.

33. And all Israel, and their elders, and officers, and their judges, stood on this side the ark and on that side, before the priest the Levites, which bare the ark of the covenant of the Lord, as well **the landborn (born again) as the Hebrew of the Hebrews**, half of them over against mount Gerizim; and half of them over against mount Ebal; as Moses the servant of the Lord had commanded before, that they should bless the people of Israel.

34. And afterward he read all the words of the law, the blessings and cursings, according to all that is written in the book of the law.

35. There was not a word of all that Moses commanded which Joshua read not before all *the congregation of Israel,* (who ate the pass-ly instance where the LXX render the Hebrew word *ger* by the Greek term *xenos*, and with this exception the word is always used to represent the Hebrew word *nokri*, or foreigner. Here it is evidently a gloss upon the passage. It was commendable to "entertain strangers" (*philoxenias*). I was a stranger (*xenos*) and ye took me in." "When saw we thee a stranger" (*xenos*)? "I was a stranger (*xenos*) and ye took me not in." "Bought the potter's field to bury strangers (*xenoi*) in." "Beloved, thou doest faithfully whatsoever thou doest to the brethren, and to (*xenoi*) strangers."

Ittai the Gittite and Ruth the Moabitess were *xenoi*—pious "Gentiles" or foreigners, who were "*xenoi* from the covenants of promise."]

23. The land shall not be sold for ever; for the land is mine: for ye are **landborn** (*gerim*, Heb. —*proselutos*, Sept.) and **dwellers** (*toshabhim*, Heb.—*paroikoi*, Sept.) with me (Lev. xxv).

[See other references to the "proselytes of habitation" or resident landborns, on page 62, Section III. In the remaining references the LXX vary their

power, seeing he hath dealt deceitfully with her.

9. And if he have betrothed her unto his son, he shall deal with her after the manner of daughters (Ex. xxi).

10. For thy violence against thy brother Jacob, shame shall cover thee, and thou shall be cut off for ever.

11. In the day that thou stoodest on the other side, in the day that the strangers (*zarim*) carried away captive his forces, and **foreigners,** (*--nokr.allotr.*) entered into his gates, and cast lots upon Jerusalem, even thou wast as one of them.

12. But thou shouldest not have looked on the day of thy brother, in the day that he became a **foreigner**(*nokr. — allotr.*) ; neither shouldest thou have rejoiced over the children of Judah in the day of their destruction ; neither shouldest thou have spoken proudly in the day of distress (Obadiah i).

16. To deliver thee from the strange (*zar*) woman, even from the **foreigness** (*nokr.—allotr.*) which flattereth with her words (Prov. ii).

10. Lest strangers (*zarim*) be filled with thy wealth, and thy labors be in the house

SECTION VII.—REMAINING REFERENCES.

over) with the women and the little ones and the landborn (*ger — pros.*) that was conversant among them (Josh. viii).

[The close of the last verse would read literally: *the landborn that walked among the drawing near of them.* The LXX render it as they render *ger hgar* or landborn born again in Lev. xix, 34. The Hebrew words *kherebh* and *taveck* rendered indiscriminately "in the midst," "among," etc., in our English translation, renderings, putting "dweller" for "landborn," but never "landborn" for "dweller;" and, in so doing, may wish the reader to understand "a landborn and dweller" (resident landborn), or only a "dweller" (resident foreigner); but I think it more evident, that they change the terms to express other than the usual relations.]

4. I am a landborn* and dweller with you give me a possession of a burying place with of a foreigner (*nokr.—allotr.*);

20. And why wilt thou, my son, be ravished with a strange (*zarah*) woman, and embrace the bosom of a foreigness (*nokr. — allotr.*) (Prov. v.)

5. That they may keep thee from the strange (*zarah*) woman, from the foreigness (*nokr.*, Heb. — *ponearas* — wicked woman, Sept.) which flattereth with her words (Prov. vii,)

16. Take this garment that is surety for

---

* Abraham would seem to claim citizenship in that community, and in the reply, "Thou art a mighty prince among us," the sons of Heth seem to accord the claim; and if so, that is all the phrase "landborn and dweller" requires. It means substantially citizenship. The "landborn and dweller" (resident landborn or "proselyte of habitation") among the Jews was a citizen of the Jewish nation—one of *the people of the land*. By a special injunction the grandchild or third generation of an emigrant family of Edom or Egypt were not to be held as foreigners or sons of outland in Israel, although not a landborn; while all the children of a family of Moab and Ammon born in the land till "their tenth generation," were held as foreigners or sons of outland. The former might be a *ger* (citizen and as a landborn) though not a landborn; the latter, though a landborn, might not be a *ger*. So Abraham's position among the sons of Heth depends entirely upon the "naturalization laws" of the sons of Heth, and they seem to accord him citizenship. Or the meaning may be: I am *as* a landborn and dweller (as a citizen of foreign parentage) with you, give me a possession of a burying place, etc. In this way we must understand the language of Moses, in reference to his relation to the Midianites, in the phrase rendered "stranger in a strange land" (Ex. ii, 22), and "alien in a strange land" (Ex. xviii, 3). And she (Zipporah) bore him a son and he (Moses) called his name Gershom (*ger—shom*, Heb.—which means a *landborn there, or citizen there*); for, said he, I have been a *ger* (landborn) in a *nokriah* (foreign) land; I have been *as* a landborn in a land in which I was not born—lived in a foreign land but not as a foreigner. Hence the name he gave his firstborn son, Gershom, a name to keep in memory Jethro's kindness in receiving him (a refugee) and giving him a wife which they were not wont to do to foreigners. I have been treated as a citizen where properly I was a foreigner. The idea is just the opposite of that contained in that plaintive expression, "a stranger in a strange land."

certainly were not so used by the Hebrews.]

9. And a man that is clean shall gather up the ashes of the heifer, and lay them up without the camp in a clean place, and it shall be kept for the congregation of the children of Israel, for a water of separation: it is a purification for sin.

10. And he that gathereth the ashes of the heifer shall wash his clothes, and be unclean until the even: and it shall be unto the children of Israel, and unto the **landborn born again** (*ger hgar*, Heb. —*pros. proskei*, Sept.) among them for a statute for ever.

20. But the man that shall be unclean, and shall not purify himself, that soul shall be cut off from among the congregation (*khahal*—church), because he hath defiled .... upon him; he is unclean (Num. xix).

9. These were the cities appointed for all the children of Israel, and for the **landborn born again** (*ger—hgar —pros—proskei*) among them, *that whosoever killeth any person at unawares* might flee thither, and not die by the hand of the avenger of blood, until he stood before the congregation (Josh. xx).

The line between Clean and Unclean.

you, that I may bury my dead out of my sight (*ger* and *toshabh*, Heb.—*paroikos* and *parepidamos*, Sept.) (Gen. xxiii).

15. For ye are **landborns and dwellers**, as were all our fathers; our days on the earth are as a shadow, and there is none abiding (*gerim* and *toshabhim*, Heb.—*paroikos* and *paroikountas*, Sept.) (1 Chron. xxix.)

13. And he said unto Abram, Know of a surety that thy seed shall be a **landborn** (*ger*—*paroikos*) in a land that is not theirs, and shall serve them; and they shall afflict them four hundred years (Gen. xv).

13. And David said unto the young man that told him, Whence art thou? And he answered, I am the son of a **landborn** (*ger—paroikos*), an Amalekite (2 Sam. i).

19. I am a **landborn** (*ger—paroikos*) in the earth; hide not thy commandments from me (Ps. cxix).

8. O the Hope of Israel, the Saviour thereof in time of trouble, why shouldest thou be as a **landborn** (*ger — paroikos*) in the land, and as a wayfaring man that turneth aside to tarry for a night (Jer. xiv).

The Middle Wall of Partition.

a stranger (*zar*) and take a pledge of him for a **foreigness** (*nokr.*, Heb.) (Prov. xx).

2. Let another (*zar*) man praise thee, and not thine own mouth; a **foreigner** (*nokr.*—*allotr.*), and not thine own lips (Prov. xxvii).

13. Take his garment that is surety for a stranger (*zar*) and take a pledge of him for a **foreigness** (*nokr.—allotr.*) (Prov. xxvii.)

2. A man to whom God hath given riches, wealth, and honour, so that he wanteth nothing for his soul of all that he desireth, yet God giveth him not power to eat thereof, but a **foreigner** (*nokr.*, Heb. — *xenos*, Sept.—Ittai the Gittite was called a *nokri* in Hebrew, but the LXX call him a *xenos*) eateth it: this is vanity, and it is an evil disease (Eccles. vi).

1. Remember, O Lord, what is come upon us; consider, and behold our reproach.

2. Our inheritance is turned to strangers (*zarim*) our houses to **foreigners** (*nokr.*, Heb. *xenos*, Sept.) (Lam. v.)

8. I am become a stranger (*zar*) unto my brethren, and a **foreigner** (*nokr.—xenos*) unto my mother's children (Ps. lxix).

SECTION VII.—REMAINING REFERENCES.

Clean	The Line between Clean and Unclean.	Unclean	The Middle Wall of Partition.	
15. These six cities shall be a refuge, both for the children of Israel, and..................		.....for the landborn (*ger—pros*) and for,......		......the dweller, resident foreigner (*toshabh*, Heb. — *paroikos*, Sept.) among them; *that every one that killeth any person unawares may flee thither* (Num. xxxv).
29. So these things shall be for a statute of judgment (the penalty appointed) to you...		......[unto all your generations (Sept. *geneas*) —your *nation*...............		......among all those who dwell with you— Heb. *moshabh* — Sept. *katoikias*). — Num. xxxv.]
30. Whoso killeth any person, etc. (See Num. xxxv. 30-34.)				
The people of the congregation.		*The people of the land.*		*The peoples of the lands.*
The circumcised.		*The uncircumcised.*		*The uncircumcision.*
				43. Any son of outland shall not eat of it (the passover) ....
...47. All the congregation of Israel shall keep it........................		. 48. And when a landborn shall be born again, and will keep the passover to the Lord, all the males to him being circumcised, then let him................		A dweller, resident foreigner (*toshabh*, Heb.—*paroikos*, Sept.) shall not eat of it (the passover, Ex. xii, 45).
.. come near and keep it, and he shall be as the Hebrew of the Hebrews of the land ..		.. for no uncircumcised landborn shall eat thereof...................		
...49. One law shall be to the Hebrew of the Hebrews and to the landborn born again in your midst (Ex. xii).				

CHAPTER III.

WHO WERE FOREIGNERS—"ALIENS IN THE COMMONWEALTH OF ISRAEL, AND STRANGERS FROM THE COVENANTS OF PROMISE."

I. In the language of the Greeks of the time of our Saviour, all were "children" who were not *allotrion*—foreigners—and all were "foreigners" who were not *children* (Matt. xvii, 25, 26. See page 47).

II. In the language of the Hebrews of the time of Moses, all were "brothers" who were not *nokri*—foreigners—and all were "foreigners" who were not "brothers" and "neighbors" (Deut. xv, 2–3; xxiii, 19, 20; xvii, 15. See page 45).

III. But beside the *nokri*, there were in that land, two other distinct classes of persons, viz.: the *ger*—*proselutos* in thy gates, and the *ger* and *azurah*. (See Deut. xiv, 21; Lev. xvii, 15, page 48.) I have pointed out, page 37, that the terms *ger* and *prosēlutos*, were applied to one that was a "brother;" hence the consistency of the above representations. There were in "olden times" "foreigners" and "children" (Matt. xvii, 25, 26), and there were "foreigners" and "brothers" (Deut. xv, 2, 3; xxiii, 19, 20; xvii, 15), and the latter term embraced the

ger and the *ger hgar*—*ger* that acts the *ger* of the Hebrews, and the *prosēlutos* and the *prosēlutos pros.* of the Septuagint, the transition between which classes can not *possibly be a transition of one of the nations to the Hebrew nation* (a *ger*, or *prosēlutos*, was a *brother*, and it is a *ger*, *prosēlutos*—*brother*—which is said, in our translation, to sojourn. See Hebrew and Septuagint, Ex. xii, 48; Num. ix, 14; xv, 14; Lev. xvii, 8; xix, 33; Ez. xiv, 7). It was one of the Hebrew nation, whom our translators supposed to be one of the nations; one of the *people of the land*, whom our translators supposed to be one of the *peoples of the lands*; a *brother*, whom our translators supposed to be the same as the *nokri*, Hebrew—*allotrion*, Septuagint —" foreigner," "which is not of thy people Israel." (See 2 Chron. vi, 32; 1 Kings viii, 41, pages 55, 57.)

The positions in the foregoing Chart are impregnable. Any son of outland—born in foreign parts—out of the Holy Land, which land was purified of blood-guiltiness by sacrifice (Deut. xix, 10—how?—see Deut. xxi, 1-9).—Any son of outland (except the third generation of a family of Edom — " thy brother "—or of Egypt, in whose land thou wast a *ger*—*prosēlutos*—*landborn*) shall not eat of it (the passover, Ex. xii, 43). The Israelitish nation, or people of the land, was separate from the peoples of the lands or nations, and none of these were permitted to enter the congregation of the Lord;—

"the heathen (nations) entered into her sanctuary, whom thou didst command that they should not enter into thy congregation—Church" (Lam. i, 10), *while* any one of " this nation," " thy people," " separated from every people "—any *ger—prosēlutos*, or landborn might, upon being circumcised, enter the congregation and keep the passover.

We wish our readers to observe, that in each remark, up to this point in this chapter, our argument is not to be construed as only referring to particular passages, but *as representative*. We present our classification by means of our Chart (44 pages of matter in solid columns), and we have embraced every possible authoritative (inspired Hebrew) reference in this classification. *We possess the land from ocean to ocean*—every reference of Hebrew and Greek, bearing upon the subject — all the ground which our Hebrew lexicons were made to cover, and sufficient of the ground which the Greek lexicons were made to cover, and make this presentation of the whole question, that our readers may see at a glance how wide of the mark lexicographers, some of them semi-infidel, have led us.

IV. Those seventy learned Jews who translated the Scriptures of the Old Testament out of the original language (Hebrew) into the Greek language, near three hundred years before the Saviour's time, accept these representations as correct, *for both languages*, in rendering uniformly the Hebrew

word *nokri*, and the variations of that word according to the usages of the Hebrew language, by *allotrion* and its various forms according to the usages of the Greek language, except using a new word—*xenos*, instead of *allotrion*, in some ten or twelve instances. (See Chart, right hand column throughout.)

Now, what is the import of this new term?

In Hebrew, Ittai the Gittite and Ruth the Moabitess are called *nokri* and *nokriah*, and the LXX, in these and eight or ten other instances, depart from their usual rendering (*allotrion*), and define them to be *xenos* and *xenea*; but Paul explains this term (Eph. ii, 12, 19) in setting forth the condition of those to whom it was applied *in time past* (under the old economy), and declares emphatically that they were not of the "commonwealth of Israel"—not of those to whom were the covenants of promise (*xenoi*, "from the covenants of promise"); nor fellow-citizens under that dispensation; and, in short, formed no exception to the above representations. Wherefore, says the Apostle, *remember that ye being in time past Gentiles* (Ethn.—nations) *in the flesh, who are called uncircumcision—akrobustia*—not to be circumcised, not contemplated in the covenant which God made with Abraham, of which covenant circumcision was the sign and seal of a covenant relation "betwixt me and you," and the privilege of which relation was proffered to any of the Jewish nation—"thy seed after thee in their genera-

tions." *Nations* (whom thou didst command that they should not enter thy congregation, Lam. i, 10) who are said not to be contemplated in the covenant by those contemplated in it, viz.: *that which is called the circumcision in the flesh made by hands—the Jewish nation;* that is, the Jews said, the Gentiles or nations, had no interest in the covenant—" not meet to take the children's bread and cast it to dogs."

" *That at that time* (under the old economy) *ye were without Christ* (without the " oracles of God "), *being aliens* (*apo-allotriomenoi*—held to be *allotrion*—foreigners) *from the commonwealth of Israel* (" from which sons of outland, the seed of Israel separated themselves") *and strangers* (*xenoi,* guests—Gaius, mine host, *xenos*—in a national sense, of a people to whom were the covenants of promise) *from the covenants of promise* (such as Ittai the Gittite, Ruth the Moabitess, and Cornelius the "dweller," a man fearing God, and of good report among all the *nation* of the Jews), *having no hope* (no promises held out to them in the covenant with Abraham, but "outcast of Israel," whom God shall " gather with his gathered," in the great day—Isai. lvi, 8; xi, 12; Ps. cxlvii, 2), *and without God* (a " people not my people" disowned of God) *in the world.*"

But when Christ came and brake down the " middle wall of partition," and the Gentiles (*nations*) were brought nigh and that prophetic day had arrived, when in the same place in which it had been

said, ye are not my people; there it is now said, "ye are the children of the living God." *Now, therefore, ye are no more strangers—xenoi—*more guests of a people to whom were the covenants of promise. They were of *the peoples of the lands*, and therefore could not become one of *the people of the land* (landborn); were of the nations, and could not therefore be one of "this nation," "thy people;" much less, could they be of their households. To them the Pharisees denied a "Christian burial;" "bought the potter's field to bury *xenoi* in." They were those with whom Peter ate to the horror of his fellow-disciples, until he had explained to them the vision of the great sheet, and they understood, what in other ages was not made known, that God was about to grant unto the Gentiles (nations) repentance (covenant promises of life upon repentance) unto life, and that they were about to become "fellow-heirs and of the same body and partakers of his promises in Christ by the Gospel." *Now, therefore, ye are no more xenoi and foreigners — paroikoi —* dwellers. Pious Gentiles could only be dwellers (resident foreigners) among the Jews under the old economy—not fellow-citizens. A *paroikos*—dweller—shall not eat of it (the passover, Ex. xii, 45, Septuagint), but a *ger* and *toshabh*—a *prosēlutos* and *paroikos*—a "proselyte of habitation"—or landborn and dweller, was a brother, of whom they might not exact usury (Lev. xxv, 35-37). The one was a resident foreigner, the other

was a resident landborn; the latter was a citizen of "the commonwealth," the former was not.

The ordinance of the passover corresponds entirely to these representations: Any son of outland shall not eat of it (the passover, Ex. xii, 43). A *dweller*, resident foreigner (*toshabh*, Hebrew—*paroikos*, Septuagint) shall not eat of it (the passover, Ex. xii, 45).

The LXX apply the term *xenos* to certain well-known, "God-fearing" persons, who were *nokri*—foreigners—of the peoples of lands or nations; and Paul says, the nearest approach, under the old economy, that the Gentiles (nations) could make, was to be held as *allotrion* — foreigners—by "the commonwealth of Israel," and to live as *xenoi*—guests (of or among a people—the Jewish nation, to whom were the covenants of promise) of the covenants of promise (Eph. ii, 12). The LXX then use *xenos* instead of *allotrion*, to distinguish between "God-fearing" foreigners, or pious men of the nations, and those who did not fear God; and *this is the import of this new term concerning which we proposed to inquire, and our positions are sustained,* viz.: That all who were not "children" or "brothers," were *allotrion* of the Septuagint, and *nokri* of the Hebrew—*foreigners*—and also the converse. The term *xenos*, as applied to Ittai the Gittite, Ruth the Moabitess, etc., expresses a somewhat different relation to Israel than the usual word *allotrion;* but still they were *allo-*

trion (Greek) and *nokri* (Heb.), as opposed to *children* and *brothers* (Matt. xvii, 25, 26; Deut. xv, 2, 3). Paul, in repeating his statement in Eph. ii, 19, explains, Ex. xii, 45, A *paroikos* shall not eat of it (the passover, Septuagint). "Christ having come, ye are no more (as they had been up to this time) *xenoi* (guests of that people or nation to whom were the covenants of promise) and foreigners—*paroikoi*—*dwellers* (resident foreigners), but fellow-citizens of the saints and of the household of God," etc.; none of which privileges were extended to them *in time past*. Not that God is a respecter of persons, for "in *every nation* he that *feareth him* and worketh righteousness is accepted of him" (Acts x, 34, 35). Not that God had not cared for them; he had appointed them a place in his house, "the court of the nations." Here the *xenoi*—"strangers from the covenants of promise," "in time past" *worshiped;* and although without hope in the covenant with Abraham, they were not without hope in the uncovenanted mercy of God. In answer to the complaint of the son of outland in Isai. lvi, 3, "that the Lord hath utterly separated me from his people," the prophet, after intimating the privilege which all men had of "loving the Lord," "keeping his Sabbaths," "taking hold of his covenant," declares in God's name that such "I will bring to my holy mountain and make them joyful in my house of prayer; their burnt-offerings and their sacrifices

shall be accepted upon mine altar; for my house shall be called a house of prayer for *all peoples*" (Septuagint, nations). The Lord God which gathereth the *outcast of Israel* (*Israel*, not of the covenant Israel) saith, yet will I gather others to him besides those gathered (in the covenant with Abraham) unto him (Isai. lvi, 7, 8).

Then I understand the ordinance of the passover to mean: Any son of outland (of foreign birth and associations) shall not eat of it (the passover, Ex. xii, 43). A dweller (resident foreigner, of foreign birth, but not of foreign associations) shall not eat of it (Ex. xii, 45); "shall not eat of it," even though with Ruth exclaiming, "Thy people shall be my people, thy God my God;" or with Ittai unto king David: As the Lord liveth, and as my "lord the king liveth, surely in what place my lord the king shall be, whether in death or in life, even there also will thy servant be." These, the LXX, say were *xenos* and *xenea*, and Paul " *xenoi* from the covenants of promise"—outcast of Israel, whom God shall gather with his redeemed, " the accepted of him," "of all nations, and kindreds, and *peoples* and *tongues.*"

I say, then, that the representations of Moses' time in Hebrew; the representations of the Saviour's time in Greek; the uniform rendering by the LXX of the Hebrew into Greek; with some ten or a dozen variations; Paul's explanations of those variations;

the ordinance of the passover answering back completely to these representations: all these concurring, and the explanations given one of the other, in the foregoing, *point to our conclusions, without a single drawback.* The *ger—prosēlutos*—which "shall sojourn"—*come and dwell* (Ex. xii, 48), was "a brother," one already "of the commonwealth of Israel," was not a "stranger from the covenants of promise," as were all foreigners; but upon being born again and receiving an ordinance expressive of a *covenant relation*, into which new relation he entered of his own voluntary act, he was, under that dispensation, in covenant with God and a "fellow-citizen of the saints and of the household of God," and had "an inheritance among them that are sanctified." (See Ezek. xlvii, 22, 23.) Not so "in time past," the *nokri, allotrion, xenos—foreigner*, whatever might have been their character, they were aliens from the commonwealth of Israel and if pious, "strangers from the covenants of promise" (Eph. ii, 12), and could only be up till that time strangers and dwellers (resident foreigners) (Eph. ii, 19).

Dr. Alexander's rendering of the Hebrew phrase *ben nekar*—son of outland, in Ps. xviii, 45, 46, and Isai. lxii, 8, made and published more than fifteen years ago, can be sustained substantially, although so far as I know, he lived and died unconscious of the issue himself had made with the common English translation, and from that rendering follows

inevitably the logic of the ordinance of the passover, as traced on page 50, and with it much falls to the ground which hitherto has passed for truth.

I only observe here, as properly belonging to this Chapter, that the foundation of the so-called Bible servitude, or the doctrine that the Jews bought and held *foreigners* for "servants" or "bondmen," is swept out of existence; and with it must fall the false theories of those who have been prime movers (see late work, "Church and the Rebellion," by Dr. R. L. Stanton) in that rebellion which has deluged our land with blood. In consequence of this false interpretation of the Bible, *this perversion of God's truth*, and the folly into which it has led us, there is a great cry in the land—mourning for the *firstborn brave* of the land—mourning in every house for husbands, or brothers, or sons, or wives and children, or for friends and neighbors.

It will not be denied, that circumcision was the ordinance of introduction into the Jewish Church, and that only those who were to be permitted to enter the congregation and enjoy its privileges were to receive this ordinance. The declaration, that such and such a class of persons shall not enter the congregation of the Lord, is equivalent to the declaration, that that class of persons shall not eat the passover. All the congregation of Israel shall keep it (Ex. xii, 47); and, of course, those who shall not *enter* shall not *keep*. The saying, that any

son of outland shall not eat of it (the passover, Ex. xii, 43), is only saying, that he shall not enter the congregation of the Lord; and the saying (Lam. i, 10), that "the nations (Hebrew, *goyim*—Septuagint, *ethn.*) whom thou didst command that they should not enter thy (*khahal*, Hebrew—*ecclesia*, Septuagint) congregation," is only saying that God commanded that "the nations" should not eat of the passover; so of the first and second generation of Edom, "thy brother," etc.; so also of Moab and Ammon till the tenth generation—the first and second of the one and till the tenth of the other, shall not eat of the passover—"shall not enter the congregation of the Lord." These were the "uncircumcision"—aliens from the commonwealth of Israel, and strangers from the covenants of promise.

We only ask, for our present purpose, *that it be admitted* that the persons termed *miqnath keseph*— "bought for money"—at least *might* enter the congregation of the Lord and eat the passover (but every man's servant *bought for money*, etc., shall eat thereof, Ex. xii, 44); and if so, the following are the only possible renderings of the passages where the expression, "bought with money," is connected with the terms son of outland, nations, etc. Gen. xvii, 12, must be read, "he that is bought with thy money, descended of any son of outland which is not of thy seed"—a question of *seed, lineage, stock*— and this particular reference is to the "bought for

money," of "stock" not "of Israel," or more properly not of (Eber) the Hebrews. For this use of *min*, see Gesenius' Hebrew Lexicon, 2, (*b*) — Kings shall be of her—"descended of" her, Gen. xvii, 16. The Lord give thee seed of this woman— "descended of" this woman (1 Sam. ii, 20).

The son of outland might neither enter the congregation of the Lord nor eat the passover; "the bought with money" *might* do both; hence, the above is the only rendering possible, or you make the Bible contradict itself. Again, Gen. xvii, 27, must be read: And all the men of his house born in his house, and "the bought with money" (*min-eth*—two Hebrew prepositions joined together), "descended of," and "separated from" a son of outland, were circumcised with him. And again, Lev. xxv, 44, must be read: "Both thy bondmen and bondmaids which thou shalt have shall be" "descended of" and "separated from" the nations round about, etc. (The particular reference here in the time of Moses being to the stock of nations *round about*—not of the seed of Israel—not of the seed of Canaan). We have seen that God commanded that *the nations* should not enter the congregation (Lam. i, 10), and, of course, not eat the passover; and hence this rendering, or you make the Bible contradict itself. Again, the dweller, resident foreigner (*toshabh*, Hebrew—*paroikos*, Septuagint) shall not eat of it (the passover, Ex. xii, 45). But the

"bought with money" *might*, eat the passover; hence not resident foreigners but their descendants. "Moreover (Lev. xxv, 45) of the children of the dwellers, resident foreigners (*toshabhim*, Hebrew—*paroikoi*, Sept.—plural) which do," ... "of them shall ye buy and (the children) of their families that are with you, *which they begat in your land*." While dwellers (resident foreigners) *shall not* eat of the passover (Ex. xii, 45) their children and the children of their families, which they begat in your land—here said to be the class of persons "bought with money," or that "ye shall buy"—were a class of persons which it is admitted *might* eat the passover. We must therefore admit a Biblical contradiction, or read "bought with thy money," "descended of" any son of outland (Gen. xvii, 12)—"bought with money," "descended of" and "separated from" a son of outland (Gen. xvii, 27)—"descended of" and "separated from" the nations round about (Lev. xxv, 44); and (45) "ye shall buy" the children of dwellers (resident foreigners) and (the children) of their families which they begat in your land; not the dwellers themselves—they shall not eat the passover—"were aliens in the commonwealth of Israel, and strangers from the covenants of promise;" nor the children of their families *which they begat abroad*—such would be sons of outland, and, of course, prohibited this relation within the covenant. The sons of outland, dwellers (resi-

dent foreigners), or any one of the nations were, within the commonwealth of Israel, aliens and strangers from the covenants of promise, and "*shall not eat the passover*"—"*shall not enter thy congregation.*" This is the language which the Scriptures as a mass speak; any one of *the nations,* as they used this term, was not of the Jewish *nation* to whom was proffered a covenant relation like to that made with Abraham, but was a "stranger from the covenants of promise," and entered neither the congregation nor ate the passover. To this conclusion we are forced by our understanding of the Scriptures, as set forth in the foregoing Chart.

Before this classification, that knotty question of "Bible servitude," or the doctrine, that the Jews bought and held foreigners for "servants," slaves, or "bondmen," disappears—vanishes as a preconceived opinion, which men have attempted to fasten upon the Bible, and in which attempt they have succeeded so long, only by such an indiscriminate rendering of terms as we have shown (see page 17) to exist in our English translation of the Bible.

The only renderings of the expressions rendered in our translation, "any stranger" (Gen. xvii, 12), "of the stranger" (Gen. xvii, 27), "heathen round about" (Lev. xxv, 44), are given above, that can possibly be given, so as that these expressions shall be consistent with other representations in the Bible, with reference to the class of persons referred to

under these terms. The expressions therefore of our translation, "bought with money," or "that ye buy," stand alone—severed from an associated expression which hitherto has determined its meaning—the mind of the Spirit all this time pointing, in the expression rendered "any stranger," "the stranger," "heathen round about," to a well understood fact of that economy; while we, bringing together expressions representing classes of persons antagonistic in the widest sense ("the bought with money" was "only in the Lord"—"must needs be circumcised," Gen. xvii, 12, the son of outland shall not eat the passover—shall not be circumcised) give those expressions such an interpretation as represents a system corresponding to modern Slavery, and, of course, claim the one sanctioned in the Bible as justifying the other. The principle involved and thus established by an interpretation utterly untenable, has been used to bolster up the most unjust and wicked pretenses of all modern time. Men, having no other pretense of a claim to exercise authority over their fellow-men, than usages established in a semi-barbarous age, by petty kings over serf subjects, have plead here a Bible precedent for the exercise of an authority which, having usurped, they call a "divine right," and *lesser tyrants* having no other pretense of a claim upon their fellow-men than that no less stupendous imposition—the established usages of the slave trade—

have plead a "Patriarchal" precedent and Bible sanction, for their no less preposterous usurpations. But the day has come, when it is seen that such wickedness will defeat its own ends. There is a God who hears and reigns, and "our eyes have seen" how under the mysterious workings of his providence, "the wages kept back by fraud," have been scattered to the winds, and how he punishes the guilty of the nation, and the guilty nation under whose aègis such crimes have been winked at.

There was no Bible precedent for all this folly and wickedness, which friend and foe now see to have come to an end so mysteriously and so suddenly, that neither the one nor the other can easily realize it.

The phrase rendered "bought with money," in our English translation, or "that ye buy," is a technical phrase, expressive of a relation of one "brother" to another "brother" in that nation and commonwealth of "brothers" (any one of whom was not permitted to exact usury of another, any one of whom must not refuse to lend "to thy poor brother," because "the year of release is at hand," and as a creditor must not exact that lent in the seventh year, the year of release), and *never used* to express a relation of a foreigner—a son of outland, one of the peoples of the lands or nations—to one of the Jewish nation—NEVER.

CHAPTER IV.

THE HEBREW NATION—COMMONWEALTH OF ISRAEL OR PEOPLE OF THE LAND.—(See Chart, Sec. II.)

I. *Made up " of stock of Israel"—consisting of " thy brother a Hebrew man" whom " thou shalt not hate;" and " thy neighbor" a " Hebrew of the Hebrews," whom " thou shalt love as thyself."* (See Chart, Sec. IV.)

II. *Made up " of stock" not " of Israel"—consisting of the landborn in thy gates, or a landborn and dweller, " thy brother " " whom thou shalt not hate," and the landborn born again, " thy neighbor " whom " thou shalt love as thyself."* (See Chart, Sec. III.)

Observe Chart, Sec. IV, if the Hebrew word *azurah*, which I render "Hebrew of the Hebrews," means homeborn, as generally rendered, I ask who "in Israel" "among the children of Israel"—"among you" were not homeborn? All the children of Israel were "homeborn," but all the children of Israel were not "*azurah* among the children of Israel." Evidently a class among the children of Israel were called *azurah*.

Nor can you substitute from the middle column

(Deut. xv, 12), and read "thy brother an Hebrew man" "among the children of Israel." Because (1) all were "brothers" who were not "foreigners" (see Section I, page 45, Deut. xv, 3); and (2), all the "children of Israel" evidently *were* Hebrew men, or men of the Hebrew nation, and the latter could not be used to define a part of the former. To speak of a man of the Hebrew nation among the "children of Israel" would be a meaningless use of language. The ger that acts the ger thou shalt love as thyself (Lev. xix, 34); but remember the *ger* was a "brother," as we have seen, and the ger acting the ger more—the former thou shalt not hate—the latter thou shalt love as thyself. The latter ate the passover, the former did not. Shall we read, thou shalt not hate "thy brother a Hebrew man," and the "stranger that sojourneth" *thou shalt love as thyself?* The *azurah* was a class "among the children of Israel"—"in Israel"—"among you," a class among brethren of "the stock of Israel;" or in other words, there were two classes of the Jewish nation, so far as that nation was made up of "the stock of Israel," viz.: the *azurah* who was of "the people of the congregation," who was *clean* and *ate the passover*; and "the Hebrew man thy brother," who was only of the Hebrew nation, who was *unclean* and did not eat the passover, was only of "the people of the land." Paul was "of the stock of Israel, of the tribe of Benjamin," and was more

than "a Hebrew man thy brother;" more than of the Hebrew nation, he was a Hebrew of the Hebrews, a member of the Hebrew Church, of Hebrew stock.

As a member of the Hebrew church, was Paul preeminent? What of the prophets Isaiah, Samuel, of king David; were they not as eminent as Paul the persecutor? They, each one, were a Hebrew of the Hebrews "in Israel"—Hebrew of the Hebrews "among the children of Israel," as well as Paul— as well as every one of "the people of the land," of "the stock of Israel," who was of "the people of the congregation."

The expression, "thy brother a Hebrew man," served to distinguish a brother "of the stock of Israel" from "thy brother" a landborn and dweller, or the landborn in thy gates, of "stock" not "of Israel;" and very evidently all these classes are referred to in Deut. xv, 7, 11 :—" If there be among you a poor man of *any of thy brethren* (comprehending: 1, 'thy brother a Hebrew man;' 2, the landborn and dweller 'thy brother;' 3, and the landborn or *ger, proselutos*—both of which terms are equivalent to the term brother—in thy gates) *within any of thy gates in thy land* which the Lord thy God giveth thee, thou shalt not harden thy heart nor shut thy hand against *thy poor brother.*"

"But thou shalt open thy hand wide unto him, and

shalt surely lend him sufficient for his need, in that which he wanteth.

"Beware that there be not a thought in thy wicked heart, saying, The seventh year, the year of release, is at hand; and thine eye be evil against *thy poor brother*, and thou givest him naught; and he cry unto the Lord against thee, and it be sin unto thee.

"Thou shalt surely give him, and thy heart shall not be grieved when thou givest unto him; because that for this thing the Lord thy God shall bless thee in all thy works, and in all that thou puttest thy hand unto. For the poor shall never cease *out of the land;* therefore I command thee, saying, Thou shalt open thine hand wide unto *thy brother, to thy poor, and to thy needy in thy land.*"

The allusions in this passage are very frequent, if you understand it to refer to "*any brother,*" a landborn (*a brother*), *a landborn in the gates* (*a brother*), "*landborn and dweller thy brother,*" and "*thy brother an Hebrew man.*" Confusion on this subject is altogether unnecessary. There were two classes of *prosēlutoi*; the *prosēlutos* and *prosēlutos pros.* of the Sept., and the *ger* and the *ger* that acts the *ger* of the Hebrew; and the one upon being circumcised drew near and ate the passover, and became the other. Men who draw their ideas from existing translations, are not able to tell *you anything about the so-called two classes of proselytes.*

To show the confusion that exists in relation to

this subject, I quote from the *Encyclopedia of Religious Knowledge*, article—*Proselyte:* "Many are of the opinion that there appears to be no ground whatever for this distinction of proselytes of the gate and proselytes of righteousness." Many doubt the existence of such classes of persons. Our Chart ought to convince such that there were two classes of *proselutoi*, at least. Dr. Tomline, as quoted in the same work, says: "Proselytes were those, and those only, who took upon themselves the obligations of the whole Mosaic law, but retained that name till they were admitted into the congregation of the Lord as adopted children. Gentiles were allowed to worship and offer sacrifices to the God of Israel in the outer court of the temple; and some of them, persuaded of the sole and universal sovereignty of the Lord Jehovah, might renounce idolatry without embracing the Mosaic law; *but such persons appear to me never to be called proselytes in Scripture or in any ancient Christian writer.*"

The last sentence is just as I represent it; but observe, the two sentences are inconsistent. According to the last sentence "Gentiles" were "*never called proselytes;*" if so, who were the "proselytes" spoken of in the first sentence? If converted Gentiles were not "proselytes," there were no "proselytes" as generally defined:—"In the language of the Jews, those were called by this name (proselyte) who came to dwell in their country, or

who embraced their religion, being not Jews by birth." The Greek term *prosēlutos*, as used by the LXX and in the New Testament, is not correctly represented by the term, "proselyte," as we use it.

On account of this misuse of the word, Dr. Tomline is not consistent with himself in the two sentences given in the article. After saying that "the proselytes were those who took upon them the obligations of the whole Mosaic law," he adds, that "Gentiles were never called proselytes in Scripture or in any ancient Christian writer," which declaration is destructive of the definition of a proselyte; that is, those who "embraced their religion not being Jews by birth." If he had said that "Gentiles (nations) were allowed to worship and offer sacrifices to the God of Israel in the outer court of the temple" ("court of the Gentiles" or nations); and then said that the "descended of any son of outland" (Gen. xvii, 12)—or the "descended of" and "separated from" a son of outland (Gen. xvii, 27)—or the "descended of" and "separated from" the nations round about (Lev. xxv, 44), or the children of dwellers (resident foreigners) and (the children) of their families which they begat in your land (Lev. xxv, 45), who, when joined to you, were of your nation and were called *prosēlutoi*—not born to the nations in their land, but "your come by birth in your land,"—and that such *prosēlutoi* or *landborns* as "took upon themselves

the obligations of the whole Mosaic law" "were admitted into the congregation of the Lord as adopted children," *the statement would have been consistent* and correct. To Dr. Tomline's statement, that "such persons (pious Gentiles) appear to me never to be called *proselytes* in Scripture, or in any ancient Christian writer," I add Dr. Lardner's statement, viz.: "I do not believe that the notion of two sorts of Jewish proselytes can be found in any Christian writer before the fourteenth century or later."

It would seem that in that century, when much of religion was form, it was considered legitimate to modernize a Greek word and attach a religious meaning to it; hence we have a word with such a meaning to it which the LXX uniformly use in rendering the original of the word "stranger," in the expression we render "stranger shall sojourn" (Ex. xii, 48, and elsewhere), the one in no sense the equivalent of the other.

Dr. Jennings also observes that "there does not appear to be sufficient evidence in the Scripture history, of the existence of such proselytes of the gates as the Rabbins mention; nor indeed of any who with propriety can be styled proselytes, except such as fully embraced the Jewish religion."

The confusion that exists in relation to this subject will be seen by observing that according to Dr. Jennings, "there is not sufficient evidence of the

existence of such proselytes of the gate as the Rabbins mention;" according to Dr. Lardner, "the notion of two sorts of Jewish proselytes can not be found in any Christian writer before the fourteenth century or later;" and according to Dr. Tomline, "converted Gentiles might renounce idolatry without embracing the law of Moses, but such persons appear to me never to be called proselytes in Scripture or in any ancient Christian writer."

The *first* denies the existence of the proselyte of the gate. The *second* denies the existence of the notion of two sorts of proselytes before the fourteenth century. The *third* denies *the existence of any kind whatever of proselytes, that is* "converted Gentiles, called proselytes," as the word proselyte has been defined to mean, but says that "proselytes were those and those only who took upon themselves the obligation of the whole Mosaic law."

The truth is very simple; converted Gentiles, or converts of the nations, were never called *prosēlutoi;* but there *were* two classes of *prosēlutoi* (see Chart, middle and left hand column), and they were both of the Jewish *nation* or of "the people of the land;" and the "*prosēlutos* in thy gates" who "took upon himself the obligations of the whole Mosaic law," "was admitted into the congregation of the Lord," and then "with propriety could be styled" a "religious *prosēlutos.*" The *landborn* or one of "the

people of the land " thus became one of the "people of the congregation."

The article in the *Encyclopedia*, from which I have quoted, begins: "PROSELYTE (*prosēlutos*) signifies *a stranger, a foreigner;* the Hebrew word *ger,* or *nekar,* also denotes one who comes from abroad or from another place." Now, these words, *ger* and *nekar,* are just as distinct as Jew and Gentile. The Middle Wall of Partition ran between the classes of persons so called (see Chart throughout), and not in one solitary instance do the LXX render *nekar prosēlutos,* or *ger allotrion,* while *ger* is rendered once, and once only, *xenos* (Job xxxi, 32); and *nekar* is rendered perhaps a dozen of times by the term *xenos.* The difference between the two words is, that every *ger* was a *brother,* while every *nekar* was a *foreigner.* The reader will see that the light which the above rays of *Religious Knowledge* shed upon the question in hand is of *very doubtful character.*

But again: all Rabbinical tradition says that there were two classes of proselytes (*prosēlutoi,* we suspect); one belonging to the Jewish Church, the other belonging to the Jewish nation, or one class circumcised and eating the passover, the other not circumcised nor eating the passover; these can be no other than the *ger* and *ger acting the ger* of the Hebrew and the *prosēlutos* and *prosēlutos pros.* of the Septuagint; one of them of "the people of the congregation," the

other of "the people of the land." "The proselytes in the gates," the Rabbins say, "without obliging themselves to circumcision or to any other ceremony of the law, feared and worshiped the true God, observing the rules imposed on Noah. These were, according to the Rabbins: 1. To abstain from idolatry (2d commandment); 2. From blasphemy (3d com.); 3. From murder (6th com.); 4. From adultery (7th com.); 5. From theft (8th com.); 6. To appoint just and upright judges (shared in the appointment of civil officers); 7. Not to eat of the flesh of any animal cut off while it was alive."—*Encyclopedia of Religious Knowledge.*

I. *I observe that the king-making and deposing power were "the people of the land."*

The so-called proselytes of the gate were not of "the peoples of the lands," or "sons of outland," from whom the seed of Israel separated themselves, and they were not of "the people of the congregation," because they were not circumcised; but they did share in the elective franchise—in the appointment of civil officers (judges), and were therefore of the commonwealth of Israel, or of "the people of the land," and joined in appointing and deposing kings. (See Chart, Sec. II.) It will be observed above, that five of the so-called "rules imposed on Noah" are nothing more nor less than so many of the ten commandments; and I propose to point out, very briefly, in the Bible itself, the obligations that were

laid upon both these "sorts of proselytes," as citizens of "the commonwealth" or as being of "the people of the land" (not sons of outland), to keep the whole law of the ten commandments, and to join in the execution of the penalties which they were required to visit upon the violators of this law.

The reader will constantly bear in mind, that the Hebrews, in using the expression "people of the land," embraced both of the so-called "classes of proselytes," or the *ger* and the *ger* acting the *ger*, which classes the LXX represent by the Greek terms *prosēlutos* and the *prosēlutos pros.* (the former of which upon being circumcised, became the latter), and which classes in our English translation, are represented or rather *misrepresented* by the terms "stranger" and "stranger that sojourneth," while, in fact, any son of outland or "stranger that sojourneth" was not permitted to eat the passover.

First Commandment. The man enticing you to have another "God before me;" "namely, of the gods of the *peoples*" "thou shalt stone him with stones that he die," "thine hand shall be first upon him to put him to death, and afterwards the hand of *all the people*" (Deut. xiii, 7, 10). But *all the people* are said to do, in 2 Chron. xxiii, 17, what *all the people of the land* are said to do in 2 Kings xi, 18 (compare also Jer. xxxiii, 10, 17); so that the expressions *all the people* and *all the people of the land* are

equivalent; but *the people of the land,* or *all the people of the land,* were citizens of the commonwealth of Israel or the Hebrew nation (see Chart, Sec. II), embracing both classes of *prosēlutoi*—the clean and the unclean of "stock" not "of Israel."

Second Com. "If there be among you, *within any of thy gates* (covering at least the *brother—*a *ger—prosē-lutos* in thy gates) which the Lord thy God giveth thee *a man or woman,* that hath gone and served other gods, thou shalt bring forth that man or that woman and shalt stone them with stones till they die; at the mouth of two witnesses or three witnesses shall he that is worthy of death be put to death; but at the mouth of one witness he shall not be put to death. The hands of the witness shall be first upon him to put him to death and afterwards the hands of *all the people*" (Deut. xvii, 1, 7). The civil *Israel,* of whom was the proselyte of the gate, who, according to tradition also, must "abstain from idolatry."

Third Com. "And the Israelitish woman's son blasphemed *the name of the Lord* and cursed." "And the Lord spake unto Moses, saying, Bring forth him that cursed without the camp; and let all that heard him (the witnesses) lay their hands upon his head and let all the congregation (Sept., synagogue) stone him. And thou shalt speak unto the children of Israel, saying, Whosoever curseth his God shall

bear his sin. And he that blasphemeth the name of the Lord, he shall surely be put to death, and all the congregation (Sept., synagogue) shall certainly stone him; as well [the landborn (born again) as the Hebrew of the Hebrews] when he blasphemeth the name of the Lord shall be put to death" (Lev. xxiv, 11, 16). "All the congregation (Sept., synagogue) shall stone with stones the man," etc., whether one of the nation or of the Church, and if of the Church, whether of Jew or Gentile "stock," high or low, shall be put to death: "Whosoever curseth his God shall bear his sin," and "let all that heard (witnesses) lay their *hands upon his head*," etc.. But, as just quoted, in reference to the *second commandment*, the hands of the witnesses shall be first upon him to put him to death, and afterwards the hands of *all the people*—meaning the civil Israel which embraced the "two sorts of proselytes."

Fourth Com. "And while the children of Israel were in the wilderness they found a man that gathered sticks upon the Sabbath day, And they that found him gathering sticks brought him unto Moses and Aaron, and unto all the congregation (Sept. synagogue). And they put him in ward because it was not declared what should be done to him. And the Lord said unto Moses, the man shall be surely put to death; all the congregation (Sept., synagogue) shall stone him with stones without the

camp. And all the congregation (Sept., synagogue) brought him without the camp and stoned him with stones, and he died (Num. xv, 32–36). Among those who shall "not do any work" on the Sabbath is "the stranger (*ger*) in thy gates" (Ex. xx, 10); and Dr. Tomline, quoted above, observes, that the "term *proselytes of the gate*, is derived from an expression frequent in the Old Testament; namely, "the stranger that is within thy gates." *Hence, the duty to observe was national—was binding upon the nation as well as the Church.*

I observe, *first*, upon the 32d verse, that the *children of Israel* were not all of the Jewish Church: And when a *ger* would act the *ger*, etc. (Ex. xii, 48), he drew near and kept the passover, and became as the *azurah* of the land; but we have seen that the " *Azurah, or Hebrew of the Hebrews, among the children of Israel*," were only a part of the children of Israel; hence the expression in the 32d verse, " children of Israel," means more than the (*khahal — ecclesia*) Church. The same expression, *children of Israel*, is used in reference to the third commandment— " speak unto the *children of Israel* and say, whosoever curseth his God," etc.; hence again, this expression (children of Israel) means more than the Church.

I observe, *second*, upon Ex. xii, 47, All the *congregation* (Heb., *gadath*—Sept., *sunagoogea*) *of Israel* shall keep the passover; that it is a question whether " Israel" limits " congregation" or " congregation "

"Israel." We have the expression, "all are not Israel which are of Israel"—evidently meaning all are not *true* Israelites who are of the "stock of Israel" or "Israelites after the flesh." "They which are the children of the flesh, these are not the children of God" (Rom. ix, 6, 9)

Now, observe, in the five instances above it is *all the congregation* (Heb., *gadath*—Sept., *sunagoogea*) shall punish the violators of the third and fourth commandments. But Samson found a synagogue (the Heb. and Sept. have the same word—*gadath*—*sunagoogea*—as in the above) of bees in the carcass of the lion (Judges xiv, 8). So also we have in Ps. xxii, 16, *the congregation or synagogue* of the wicked. It would seem therefore that the expression, *All the congregation* (Sept., synagogue) is not the equivalent of the expression, *All the congregation* of Israel*

---

* I am not prepared to define this word at present. The LXX generally render it *synagogue,* but it is evident from the expression "synagogue of bees," that they made the word synagogue to mean more than we do. I may be allowed the remark, that this is one of a class of renderings in which the LXX are not very reliable. They were, perhaps, "righteous over much," in putting a difference between the *nation* and the *nations*—Jews and Gentiles— it being exactly in the line of the carnal heart and the carnal notions of the Jews of that age; but the putting a "difference between the *clean* and the *unclean*," was too personal in its application.

Again, tradition says, that the ancient synagogues were fashioned after the temple. In the temple there was (1) the holy place or tabernacle of witness; (2) the court of the Jews or Jewish nation;

(Heb., *gadath*—Sept., *sunagoogea*), which shall keep it (the passover, Ex. xii, 47). If the term "Israel" limits or defines "congregation" in Ex. xii, 47, as it would seem from what we have just said, then the expression "All the congregation," means all the Jewish *nation* as an unit (as a swarm of bees is an unit) "shall stone the man that gathered sticks on the Sabbath day;" and this agrees with the fourth commandment, which classes "the stranger in thy gates" among those who must do no work on the Sabbath day.

Fifth Com. "All the men of his city" (evidently men of civil Israel) "shall stone with stones till he die," "the stubborn and rebellious son which will not obey the voice of his father or the voice of his mother" (Deut. xxi, 18-21) — which will not "honor father or mother that his days may be long upon the land which the Lord thy God giveth thee."

Sixth Com. These six cities shall be a refuge *for the children of Israel* (commonwealth as made up of " the stock of Israel," comprehending " the Hebrew of the Hebrews" and " the Hebrew man thy

---

and, (3) the court of the Gentiles or nations. Then the expression, "all the congregation or synagogue shall stone," etc., properly means not only all the Jewish nation or people of the land, but "pious Gentiles or dwellers" (resident foreigners), who worshiped within the synagogue or temple, in their proper apartments, shall join in stoning with stones, etc. :—*more than our positions require.*

brother"), and for the (*ger—proselutos*) landborn (commonwealth as made up of "stock" not "of Israel"), and for the dweller, resident foreigner (Heb., *toshabh*—Sept., *paroikos*) among them, that every one that killeth any person unawares may flee thither (Num. xxxv, 15). Resident foreigners or pious Gentiles—"God-fearing" men of the nations, "not called proselytes in the Bible or by any ancient Christian writer,"—enjoyed the protection of law in that commonwealth although living as aliens in the "commonwealth of Israel and strangers from the covenants of promise." The revenger of blood himself shall slay the murderer; when he meeteth him he shall slay him (Num. xxxv, 19): that is, if he escaped not to the city of refuge. And when he that doth flee unto one of those cities and shall stand at the entering of the gate of the city (place where the civil authorities met) *and shall declare his cause* in the ears of *the elders of that city*, etc. (Josh. xx, 4). And he shall dwell in that city until he stand before the congregation (Heb., *gadath* —Sept., *sunagoogea*) for judgment (Josh. xx, 6). And the congregation (*gadath*, Heb.—*sunagoogea*, Sept.) shall judge between the slayer and the revenger of blood according to these judgments (Num. xxxv, 24). But if found guilty, who executed the sentence? We read in the same chap. (30th verse)— " Whoso killeth any person, the murderer shall be put to death by the mouth of witnesses," etc. If the

slayer escaped to the city of refuge and claimed a trial, the revenger of blood must bring his witnesses, and if found guilty " the hands of the witnesses (the revenger of blood and others) shall be first upon him to put him to death, and afterwards the *hands of all the people*" (Deut. xvii, 7). At least the whole congregation (*gadath*, Heb.— *synagogue*, Sept.) must see that the sentence was executed; but observe, it is not "the congregation of Israel," as limited.

Seventh Com. The adulteress:—" *All the men of her city* shall stone her with stones that she die" (Deut. xxii, 21); so also the adulterer and adulteress (Deut. xxii, 24). "All the men of her city," evidently means more than "all the congregation of Israel;" the requirement was therefore of the civil Israel. The *proselyte of the gate* who was not circumcised, and therefore not a member of the Jewish Church, engaged "to abstain from adultery" (tradition); the law was therefore a civil law, and binding upon the nation.

Eighth Com. If the *theft* be certainly found in his hand alive, whether it be ox or ass or sheep, he shall restore double (Ex. xx, 4). If he steal a man, " *life shall go for life;*" And he that stealeth *a man* (mattered not who) and selleth him, or if he be found in his hand (if the man purposed to sell him) he shall surely be put to death (Ex. xxi, 16)

Ninth Com. And the judges shall make diligent

inquisition; and, behold, if the witness be a false witness and hath testified falsely against "his brother" (all were "brothers" who were not "foreigners"); then shall ye do unto him as he had thought to have done unto "his brother" (Deut. xviii, 18, 19). The false witness shall make amends to him whom he sought to injure, to the full extent of his false oath. If he testified falsely against "his brother" to put him to death, "thine eye shall not pity, but life shall go for life;" if to injure "his brother" in anything short of life, "eye for eye, tooth for tooth, hand for hand, foot for foot" (Deut. xix, 21). Every citizen of the commonwealth was "a brother;" hence this law was a *law of the commonwealth or civil Israel.*

Tenth Com. "Covetousness, which is *idolatry*," was *punished with death.* See above, second commandment.

Covetousness leads *to theft:* —"Thou shalt not covet thy neighbor's house," nor his ox nor his ass;" *to adultery*—"Thou shalt not covet thy neighbor's wife," so that the covetousness which leads to the "overt act" in violation of this command, was punished with death in the *second, seventh,* and *eighth* commandments.

Rabbinical tradition says, that certain rules, which are substantially the *second, third, sixth, seventh, and eighth commandments,* were "imposed" upon "the proselytes of the gate;" and I have given evidence

from the Bible itself, going to show, with more or less conclusiveness, that the keeping the ten commandments were conditions of citizenship in that commonwealth; or, in other words, *the ten commandments in their negative requirements*—in so far as they said "*thou shalt not*,"—were civil *in their applications** (*in their requirements, and in their penalties*), to which all "the people of the land" or citizens of the commonwealth, embracing both classes of the so-called proselytes (the *ger* and the *ger acting the ger* of the Hebrew and the *prosēlutos and prosēlutos pros.* of the Septuagint) *must submit, and they must join* in the execution of the penalties of this law upon any offending citizen of the commonwealth; and more than this, upon those residing within the commonwealth: The dweller (resident foreigner) might flee to the city of refuge and claim a trial. (See Num. xxxv, 15, page 89.)

If these conclusions are correct, which we claim,

---

* In their higher sense, as applying to the heart and affections, as explained by the Saviour, they were no doubt ecclesiastical in their requirements. "Ye have heard that it was said by them of old time, thou shalt not kill; and whosoever shall kill shall be in danger of the judgment;"—put his life in jeopardy to the civil law which demanded his own life in return. "But I say unto you, that whosoever is angry with his brother ("shalt not hate thy brother in thine heart") without a cause, shall be in danger of the judgment"—of another judgment and other penalties. "But whosoever shall say thou fool, shall be in danger of hell fire;" put his soul in jeopardy—in danger of eternal damnation.

the death penalty among the Jews was a penalty, executed by *civil authorities*, upon offenders against *civil law*, and the doctrine that *the Church* has a right to exercise civil power and inflict bodily punishment, is a dogma entirely popish in its origin and character. *Such a power was never committed to the Church under the Old Testament economy, and we have no evidence that even "Phariseeism" ever dared to assume the right to exercise such a power.* Corporeal penalties, in the Jewish commonwealth were civil in their character, executed in behalf of order and the peace of civil society; the violation of any one of the ten commandments being considered a crime destructive of good order, and conduct inconsistent with the continued existence of social order among men.

II. *Ecclesiastical penalties were separation from The Church.*

(1.) *For a definite length of time.*—Every soul that eateth that which dieth of itself, or that which was torn of beasts, among the Hebrew of the Hebrews or among the landborn (born again), shall both wash his clothes and bathe himself in water, and be *unclean till even*; then he shall be clean (Lev. xvii, 15).

(2.) *For an indefinite length of time.*—But if he wash them not nor bathe his flesh then he shall bear his iniquity (Lev. xvii, 16).

If the means ordered for purification were observed the offender was restored at even; if not,

that man shall be *unclean* (not excommunicated). And the man that shall be unclean and shall not purify himself, that soul shall be "cut off" from among (from the midst of) the congregation (*khahal—Church*), because he hath defiled the sanctuary of the Lord; the water of separation hath not been sprinkled upon him; *he is unclean* (Num. xix, 20). The *khahal*, Heb.—*ecclesia*, Sept., *i. e.*, Church, consisted of the Hebrew of the Hebrews and the *ger* that acts the *ger*, or landborn born again. (See Num. xv, 16, page 76; and Ex. xii, 49, page 50.)

Seven days shall there be no leaven found in your house; for whosoever eateth that which is leavened, even that soul shall be "cut off" from (*min*) *the congregation of Israel* (*gadath*, Heb.—*sunagoogea*, Sept.), whether among the landborn (born again) or among the Hebrew of the Hebrews (Ex. xii, 19). The Church is twice referred to in the above, viz.: (1) in the expression, *the congregation of Israel:*—All *the congregation of Israel* (*gadath*, Heb.—*sunagoogea*, Sept.) shall keep it (the passover, Ex. xii, 47); and (2) the landborn when classed with the Hebrew of the Hebrews, as above, composed the Church, or *khahal*, Heb.—*ecclesia*, Sept., and were *clean*. (See in reference to "that which dieth of itself," page 48.)

The expressions "cut off from the congregation" (*khahal—Church*), and "cut off from the congregation (*gadath*, Heb.—*sunagoogea*, Sept.) of Israel," do not naturally mean more than to be separated from the

Church *as unclean*. But the man that is *clean* and is not on a journey and forbeareth to keep the passover, even the same soul shall be cut off from (*min*) his people (Num. ix, 13). The *clean*, or that member of the Church who would continue his covenant relation, must keep the passover, and the language here may only mean, cut off from the " people of the congregation " who ate the passover (see page 50); or looking upon him in the light of a "covenant breaker," it may mean more than being held as *unclean*—as one of " the people of the land "—may mean that he shall be held " as a heathen man," or as one of the nations. I have represented this to be the meaning in Chart (Sec. V, page 71). The former is perhaps correct.

(3.) *Excommunication.*—But the soul that doeth aught presumptuously, of the Hebrew of the Hebrews or of the landborn (born again), the same reproacheth the Lord, and that soul shall be cut off from among (*min kherebh—from the drawing nigh of*) his people. Because he hath despised the word of the Lord and hath broken his commandment, that soul shall *be utterly cut off* (Num. xv, 30, 31). The Lord hath *utterly separated me* (the son of outland) from his people (Isai. lvi, 3). Any son of outland shall not eat of it (the passover, Ex. xii, 43). The sons of outland were of the peoples of lands—of the *far off nations* (not of the *drawing nigh* nation); hence, to be held as *utterly separate* from the drawing

nigh of his people, is *at least* to be held as "a heathen man," or as one of the nations "whom thou didst command that they should not enter into thy congregation"—thy Church (Heb., *khahal*—Sept., *ecclesia*) Lam. i, 10. The *presumptuous despiser* of the word of the Lord, who hath broken his commandment—covenant breaker—was held *utterly separate*, as the nations were *utterly separate*—held "as a heathen man," as one of the nations; and if so, "no place could be found for a repentance unto a restoration" of the offender under that economy. God would not renew his covenant with such a "covenant breaker;" yet in *every nation* "he that feareth God and worketh righteousness is accepted of him;" and while such offenders were, with the nations of the world, to be left to the uncovenanted mercy of God, yet there was a place appointed within the walls of God's house (court of the nations or Gentiles), where the prayers of the truly penitent of them might be offered, and we are assured (Isai. lvi, 8) that God "will gather others to him (the "accepted of him in every nation") besides those that are gathered to him" (the Jewish Church of the Jewish nation). That one "cut off from his people"—"*utterly separated*"—"held as a heathen man," was not then to be received back or restored again to the Jewish Church, but that did not determine his eternal state. Such an offender, by misconduct, had forfeited a privilege which those of

that nation only enjoyed under the covenant with Abraham. This subject must be better understood before that difficult passage (Heb. vi, 4–7) can be explained. "For it is impossible—*adunaton* (things may be impossible—*adunaton*—"with men," "but with God all things are possible"—*dunata*) for those who were once enlightened, etc.," "*If they shall fall away* ('the lapsed'—the excommunicated) *to renew them again unto repentance*," or, as it may be rendered, *to restore them again upon repentance*. Can it be possible, that even in New Testament times, men, whose duty, as office-bearers in God's house, require them to form a judgment of men by their conduct, must not *restore again upon repentance*, even "with the advice and concurrence of presbytery," "the lapsed," the excommunicated, "those that fall away" or "covenant breakers," "seeing they crucify to themselves the Son of God afresh and put him to an open shame?"

If I should make the statement, that "no repentance would justify the office-bearers in God's house in restoring such an offender, and in allowing him to renew a covenant with God and his Church *once broken*," such a statement would be in exact accordance with the discipline of the Jewish Church, and such is the import of the language of the Saviour, "if he neglect to hear the Church, let him be unto thee as a *heathen* man." The early Christian Church held such a doctrine, referring to this passage of

Scripture as authorizing it; and the Council of Nice, which met A. D., 325, held that the "lapsed" (see Council of Nice, canon 11)—"those that fell away"—should only be restored to "the full communion of the Church," after *eleven years* of good conduct, and "flagrant apostates" after *fifteen years;* but the Novatians of the previous century held that "such as denied Christ" "ought never to be admitted again to the Church." "Respecting the fundamental articles of the Christian faith there was no disagreement between the *Novatians* and other Christians. Their peculiarity was that they would not receive into the Church persons who, after being baptized, fell into the greater sins." "They did not, however, exclude them from all hopes of *eternal salvation.*" (See *Mosheim's Church History*, Book I, Century III, Part II, Chap. V, Sec. 18.) The Novatians, then, taking this Scripture as authority, would *not restore again* to the Church, *even upon repentance,* "the lapsed"—"the excommunicated"—"those that fall away;" but they did not say that they could not be saved. By the law laid down for the direction of the office-bearers in God's house, "it was impossible," that is, the restoration of "covenant breakers," but with God all things are possible, even their "eternal salvation." They would not restore again to the Church those who "have tasted of the heavenly gift and were made partakers of the Holy Ghost, and have tasted the

good word of God and the powers of the world to come, *if they shall fall away"—should apostatize;* but they held them as "utterly separated" from the Church—held them as a "heathen man," or as any one of the nations were held by the Church under the Old Testament economy—left to the uncovenanted mercy of God, or as those to whom the offer of a covenant relation was not provided in the covenant with Abraham.

But to return: the object of the foregoing remarks, is not so much to define closely the discipline of the Old Testament Church, as *to show that that discipline was purely spiritual in its nature,* the lightest penalty being separation from the Church "*till even*" the severest excommunication, *i. e.*, to be cut off from the *drawing nigh* of his people, or to be held as *utterly separated* from his people, as the "sons of outland," "the peoples of the lands," or the nations, were held "utterly separate."

But where the offense was civil as well as ecclesiastical, civil as well as ecclesiastical penalties were incurred. I cite as briefly as possible two instances: "*Ye shall keep the Sabbath, therefore; for it is holy unto you. Every one that defileth it shall surely be put to death* (civil penalty inflicted by civil Israel, as we have seen); for whosoever doeth any work therein, that soul shall be cut off from the drawing nigh (*min kherebh*) of his people" (an ecclesiastical penalty), Ex. xxxi, 14. To be dealt with first by the ecclesiastical

body and then by the civil, both inflicting their severest penalties, the offense against both being of the gravest character.

Again (Lev. xx, 2–5), " Whosoever he be of the children of Israel, or of the *ger* that acts the *ger*, among Israel that giveth any of his seed unto Molech, he shall surely be put to death (civil penalty); *the people of the land* (civil Israel, see Chart, Sec. II) shall stone him with stones. And I will set my face against that man and will cut him off from the *drawing nigh* of his people (God will see to it that he shall be 'utterly separated' from his Church), because he hath given his seed unto Molech to defile *my sanctuary* and to profane my holy name. And if the *people of the land* (civil Israel) do any ways hide their eyes from the man (refuse to witness against him) when he giveth his seed unto Molech and kill him not (civil penalty), then I will set my face against that man and against his family, and will cut him off and all that go a whoring after him to commit whoredom with Molech *from the drawing nigh (min kherebh)* of his people." I have used the expression, *from the drawing nigh*, to represent the Hebrew expression *min kherebh*, which in this connection represents a *distinct body of people;* but whether in every case the expression means the *drawing near (the Church)*, or *those that may draw near (the nation)* is not so clear. The expression has other connections, sometimes

written as here, *the drawing nigh of his people*; and again, as in the following: " Great is the Holy one of Israel *among thy drawing nigh*"—*in the midst of the Church* (Isai. xii, 6).

The records of the Council of Nice, in its 11th canon, throws some light upon it: *The lapsed* (those "that fall away"—excommunicated) were "required, *first*, to do penance three years without the doors of the Church"—as it were in the court of the Gentiles, or nations, of the ancient synagogues or the temple—"*secondly*, six years in the porch among the catechumens"—the learners, as it were, in the court of the Jewish nation, the *nearest approach* one of the Jewish nation, or the unconverted, could make—"*thirdly*, to be allowed to witness (that is, to be present), but not to join in the celebration of the eucharist for two years more;"—none at least were permitted to enter the tabernacle of *witness* or *sanctuary*, except " the people of the *khahal*"—*ecclesia*—*Church*, or the "congregation of Israel." But we have seen that it was held in the third century that the lapsed "ought never to be admitted again to the Church."

Then, in the light of this canon of the Council of Nice, the expressions, "cut off from the drawing nigh of his people," or held "as a heathen man," *mean that the person so cut off* shall not be permitted to *enter the sanctuary* ("for she hath seen that the *heathen—goyim*, Heb.—*Ethn.*, Sept.—*nations* entered

into *her sanctuary* whom thou didst command that they should not enter into thy congregation"— *khahal*, Heb.—*ecclesia*, Sept.—*thy Church*, Lamentations of Jer. i, 10), *nor enter or mingle with* the Jewish nation in the "court of the Jews," where the whole body of the Jewish nation offered sacrifice. (See Sec. VI, page 76.)

If the "cut off," etc., worshiped at all, he must mingle neither with "the congregation of the Lord" (*the drawing nigh*) nor with his own nation (*who might draw near*), but with the *far off nations*—held as a "heathen man," as a *foreigner*, who could not *come nearer* than the court of the Gentiles or nations. Then, the man who "presumptuously despised the word of the Lord," having "tasted of the good word of God" and received "the token of the covenant in his flesh," should he not only neglect the duties which separated him from the Church temporarily, but trample underfoot his covenant engagements with God (apostatize), and openly league himself, as it were, *in covenant* with Satan, God would not permit his Church *to restore again such a "covenant breaker"* to a place among his covenant people, *even upon a professed repentance.* If that repentance was *real*, he was in God's hands, even his "*eternal salvation;*" but "he shall be unto thee as a heathen man"—shall not be permitted to enter and mingle with the Jewish Church in their worship in *the sanctuary*, nor mingle with those of his own

nation in their worship in the court of the Jewish nation.

Upon the expression, "brought Greeks also into the temple" (Acts xxi, 28), Poole, in his Commentary, remarks: "*Into the temple;* that is, into 'the court of the Jews,' which is so far unlawful that they might have killed a Roman if he had come in there; and every one was warned by an inscription upon the pillars (of the Middle Wall of Partition), *Mea dein allophulon entou tou agiou parienai,* that no stranger or foreigner might come into that holy place."

Josephus says: "There was in the court of the temple a wall or balustrade, breast high, with pillars at particular distances, and inscriptions on them in Greek and Latin, importing that strangers were forbidden from entering farther; here their offerings were received and sacrifices were offered for them, they standing at the barrier, but they were not allowed to approach the altar "—the altar of burnt-offerings which stood in the court of the Jewish nation.

If the man "cut off from the drawing nigh of his people" was restored again at any time, as it would seem might have been the opinion of the Council of Nice, in opposition to the Novatians, it must have been that he was permitted to enter the "court of the Jews" and mingle with civil Israel at the end of the sixth year, that *year of release* from

all civil embarassments—from exactions of money lent, etc.— and to enter again the congregation or sanctuary, where the congregation worshiped, at the forty-ninth year, " witnessing two years " (the forty ninth and fiftieth years) before eating the passover, and *again receiving an "inheritance among them that are sanctified"* * (Acts xxvi, 18).

---

* The holding of possessions of land outside " the walled cities," or " inheritances " in the earthly Canaan, seems to have been the peculiar privilege of the Jewish Church, and was to them a " shadow " of *an inheritance* in the Heavenly Canaan. " And it shall come to pass in what tribe the *ger acts the ger, or the landborn is born again,* there shall ye give him his inheritance, saith the Lord God " (the tithe or tenth of the increase of every third year was laid up " in the gates " for " the Levite, because he hath no part *nor inheritance with thee,* and *the landborn,* and the fatherless, and the widow "— see Deut. xiv, 28, 29, and xxvi, 11-15—" the Lord loveth *the landborn,* in giving him food and raiment " Deut. x, 18); Ez. xlvii, 23. See pages 67, 68.

And to this end " inheritances " seem to have been reallotted at the jubilee: " And when the jubilee of the children of Israel shall be, then shall their inheritance be put unto the inheritance of the tribe whereunto they are received: so shall their inheritance be taken away from the inheritance of the tribe of our fathers. And Moses commanded the children of Israel according to the word of the Lord, saying, The tribe of the sons of Joseph hath said well. This is the thing which the Lord doth command concerning the daughters of Zelophehad, saying, Let them marry to whom they think best; only to the family of the tribe of their father shall they marry. So shall not the inheritance of the children of Israel remove from tribe to tribe: for every one of the children of Israel shall keep himself to the inheritance of the tribe of his fathers. And every daughter that possesseth an inheritance

The Church, in that age, in which the Council of Nice (A. D., 325) met, *in modeling* their Churches after the temple, or synagogues, which were modeled

---

in any tribe of the children of Israel, shall be wife unto one of the family of the tribe of her father, that the children of Israel may enjoy every man the inheritance of his fathers. Neither shall the inheritance remove from one tribe to another tribe (at the jubilee); but every one of the tribes of the children of Israel shall keep himself to his own inheritance" (Num. xxxvi, 4-9).

Possessions purchased "in a walled city," *were perpetual*—"shall be established *forever to him* that bought it throughout his generations: it shall not go out in the jubilee" (Lev. xxv, 30); but the earthly possessions, or "inheritances," of the Church *were not perpetual:* "The land shall *not be sold forever:* for the land *is mine* (saith God); for ye (the Church) are landborns and dwellers (resident landborns) with me" (Lev. xxv, 45). That is, "ye," with me in *my land*, like the resident landborn with you *in this land*, have no possessions of land or "inheritances" that are more than temporary ("inheritances" might be sold to such a resident landborn —"a man"—for a period of time shorter than the jubilee period— "houses of the villages which have no wall" "shall go out in the jubilee," Lev. xxv, 31). The Church looking "for a city which hath foundations whose builder and maker is God," had no permanent earthly possessions of land or "inheritances" appointed them in the earthly Canaan; that abode was given them of God from time to time (from jubilee to jubilee), and was typical of a permanent even a heavenly inheritance—a "shadow" of "that house not made with hands eternal in the heavens." Men might have permanent possessions in that land surrounded by defenses ("in walled cities") of man's workmanship, but God was the defense of his Church ("for walls and bulwarks"), and under the broad canopy of heaven and under the protection of heaven's King, she was safe in her "inheritance"—*the gift of his grace.*

after the temple, and *in requiring the lapsed, the excommunicated,* or those that "fall away," to remain in the different apartments corresponding to the court of the nations, court of the (Jewish) nation, and the sanctuary, *three, six, and two years,* before joining again in the celebration of the Lord's Supper, *evidently* gave the expression, "cut off" from "the drawing nigh of his people," *such an interpretation;* but whether abating those rigors of the former economy, "which we nor our fathers were able to bear," from *six to three years,* and from *forty-nine* to *six years,* or whether they held, with the *Novatian sect,* as to its meaning under the Old Testament economy but not under the New, and gave this interpretation from some supposed fitness of things under the New economy, *is a question.* At least the Novatians held, that even under the New economy "the lapsed," or "those that fall away," *should not be restored again to the Church even upon repentance;* "not, however, excluding them from all hopes of eternal salvation." And the Council of Nice held, that *they should only* be restored to the full communion of the Church at *the end of eleven years;* and the decision of the Council is said to have been *a compromise* of a question which had disturbed the Church during that and previous centuries, and that *decision* throws light upon, or gives us their understanding of, the expressions, "let him be to thee as a heathen man," or as one of the nations—"cut off

from the drawing nigh of his people"—*separated from the Jewish Church and nation in their worship in the temple or in their synagogues.* Observe, this penalty was entirely of an ecclesiastical character, and executed by those having charge of matters pertaining to the worship in the temple.

But to return—and the reader will excuse us in so far as there is repetition—*a clear understanding is all-important.* The sons of outland—peoples of the lands, or the nations, were aliens within the commonwealth of Israel, and even if pious, were "strangers from the covenants of promise." "Gentiles were allowed to worship and offer sacrifice to the God of Israel in the outer court of the temple; but such persons appear to me never to be called 'proselytes' in Scripture or in any ancient Christian writer" (Dr. Tomline). In other words, *there were no proselytes, as we have understood that term, no converted Gentiles or converts of " the peoples of the lands," or converted foreigners, called " proselytes."*

The " people of the land," or Hebrew nation, was made up of the converted and the unconverted—the clean and the unclean of the "stock of Israel," viz.: the "*azurah* (Hebrew of the Hebrews) among the children of Israel," who ate the passover (Ex. xii, 48), and "thy brother a Hebrew man" (suspended or unclean Hebrew) and of the converted and unconverted—clean and unclean " of stock" not "of Israel," viz.: the *proselutoi* or landborn (not of

"the people of the congregation," or the Church) who upon being born again and circumcised (an ordinance defined everywhere in the Bible to mean regeneration), were termed "religious *prosēlutoi*" or landborn born again, and ate the passover with the *clean* of the "stock of Israel," viz.: "the Hebrew of the Hebrews." These two classes which ate the passover, made up that body termed "the people of the congregation" (*khahal*, Heb.—*ecclesia*, Sept.) or "the congregation (*gadath*, Heb. — *sunagoogea*, Sept.) of Israel," or "the congregation (*khahal*, Heb.—*ecclesia*, Sept.) of the Lord," or "thy congregation" (*khahal*, Heb.—*ecclesia*, Sept.). See Lev. xvi, 33; Ex. xii, 47; Deut. xxiii, 1, 2, 3, 8, and Lam. i, 10.

Observe:—The sons of outland, peoples of the lands, or the nations, were the *born abroad*—born outside the Holy Land or the limits of the nation. The people of the land, or the Hebrew nation, were all *homeborn*, in the sense of "born in the country;" there were therefore, besides the *azurah* (in our translation rendered "*homeborn*," in Ex. xii, 49—"born in the land," in Num. xv, 30—"Israelites born," in Lev. xxiii, 42—"born in the country," in Ez. xlvii, 22—"him that is born," in Num. xv, 30—"one of your own country," in Lev. xxiv, 22—"of your own nation," in Lev. xviii, 26), (1) "thy brother a Hebrew man" who was "homeborn" or "born in the land;" and (2), the landborn born again, also, of

course, "homeborn" or "born in the land" or "country;" and (3), the landborn (*homeborn* also) of whom there were in Solomon's time, "*one hundred and fifty thousand and three thousand and six hundred*" (2 Chron. ii, 17, see page 53). All "the people of the land" were "homeborn," or "born in the country," and all, unless by a special prohibition, such as that relating to Moab and Ammon, were reckoned as such, who were born within the limits of the nation, and chose such associations. These classes composed the nation or "the people of the land." The nation or the citizens of the nation ("people of the land") made and unmade kings (see Chart, Sec. II), performed military duty—officers "mustered the people of the land" (2 Kings xxv, 19, and Jer. lii, 25). All these classes were embraced in the expression in the covenant with Abraham (Gen. xvii, 9) "thy seed after thee *in their generations*" (see Num. xv, 14, 15, page 76; and Num. xv, 2, 3; Deut. xxix, 22, page 78). All others were aliens in the commonwealth (not citizens) and "strangers from the covenants of promise"—no one of "the people of the land" was a "stranger from the covenants of promise."

A proselyte has been defined to be one of the nations or peoples of the lands, or a Gentile "converted to Judaism," whereas such ("such appear never to be called proselytes in Scripture or in any ancient Christian writer"—Dr. Tomline) are

hereby shown not to have been so called. What shall we therefore do with the modern term, "proselyte," as thus defined? There were two classes of *prosēlutoi* (see page 50); "one of them circumcised and the other not," just as we have been accustomed to read concerning the so-called "proselytes of the gate" and "proselytes of righteousness;" but the *prosēlutoi* were not foreigners, but of foreign *descent or parentage*—of "stock" not "of Israel." The Greek term *prosēlutos*, from which our word "proselyte" is derived, of itself, neither means a *converted foreigner* nor a *converted citizen*, but is a term used entirely in a civil sense. Shall we therefore continue to say "proselyte," understanding the term to represent one class of persons, when, in fact, it represents not only an opposite class, but that opposite class of a different character? If we use the term "proselyte" as meaning a converted foreigner, it does not represent the ancient *prosēlutos* of either class; and shall we call a class (converted foreigners) "proselytes," which the ancients never called *prosēlutoi? The use of the word in this modern sense works nothing but confusion.* Over and over again is it said, ye were landborns (*ger*, Heb.— *prosēlutos*, Sept.) in the land of Egypt. They were not converts or proselytes to the Egyptian religion. Pharaoh speaks of them as *the people of the land* (Ex. v, 5). So in Israel every *ger* (Heb.) or *prosē*-

lutos (Sept.) was "a brother" and of "the people of the land," as opposed to "the peoples of the lands," who were foreigners. The LXX, in their translation of the Old Testament Scriptures, use the term *prosēlutos* very frequently (See Chart). In our English version of the Old Testament Scriptures the term "proselyte" does not occur, but in the New Testament, the Greek term *prosēlutos* is rendered "proselyte," and in consequence we have the expression *religious proselyte*, as though there were "proselytes" (converts) not *religious*. This assuming, as our translators do, that the LXX did not know how to render the Hebrew noun *ger*, and erred in hundreds of instances in rendering it *prosēlutos*, is an unwarrantable assumption. They pass, with an indifference almost absolute, a version of the Bible made by Hebrews themselves into Greek, when both the Hebrew and Greek languages were living languages! The reader will have noticed, so far as referred to in this work, with what uniformity the LXX use a particular word in Greek to represent a particular word in Hebrew, especially in the matter of common names, and in this respect, their version is undoubtedly reliable. In addition to those heretofore given, take another instance by which we have been led into confusion by our translators: The LXX render the Hebrew word *goy* or *goyim* (plural) perhaps without exception, by

the singular and plural of the Greek word *Ethnos*. The singular ought to be rendered *nation* and the plural *nations*—not *people, Gentiles, heathen,* as we have it rendered in our translation. The terms " Gentiles " and " heathen " are modern terms, and if used to mean anything more than the term *nation* or *nations,* they express more than the original, and are therefore just as improper as if they failed to express the full meaning of the original. Shall we read, " consider that this nation "—*this people—this Gentile—this heathen,* " is thy people ?" " What nation like thy people"—not *what Gentile—what heathen like thy people !* " Ye shall be unto me a holy nation "—not *holy Gentile* nor *holy heathen!* There were " men fearing God" of *the nations,* of " good report among all *the nation* of the Jews," while there were those of the *Jewish nation* " who profaned God's holy name among the *heathen* " (*nations*), —" For the name of God is blasphemed among the Gentiles (*nations*) through you." If our translation is correct, then many of the Old Testament worthies, such as Melchisedeck and Job and Hobab, Ittai the Gittite, Ruth the Moabitess, Rahab, and perhaps Elisha the Tishbite (*tishbhi*)—*the dweller* " of the inhabitants of Gilead," and many others, " the elect of the nations," would be properly termed " *heathen*," not to speak of the " fullness of the Gentiles " (nations) who now are being " brought in."

The confusion of terms is such, that the author, after repeated attempts, despairs of making further progress without adopting, to some extent, his own terms. If I use the terms now in use, "proselyte of the gate" and "proselyte of righteousness," my readers will understand me as referring to two classes of persons of foreign birth; whereas I should be talking of persons which were not foreign born. If I quote Rabbinical tradition, respecting the "proselytes of the gate" and "proselytes of righteousness," the reader will also understand the Rabbins to refer to persons of foreign birth; whereas their language is correct, in many respects, if you understand it as referring to the two sorts of *prosēlutoi* of the Septuagint, neither of which were foreign born. I think the reader will see, that any rendering of names which does not indicate whether the person was one of "the peoples of the lands," or of "the people of the land," or of "the people of the congregation," is a defective translation; and if I am to be understood, I must be allowed to use terms which will at least indicate to the reader to which of these general classes the person I may refer to belongs. This much, I think, is essential to further progress, and I shall hereafter, even in quoting tradition, generally use the expressions, "landborn in the gates" and "landborn born again," instead of "proselyte of the gates" and "proselyte of righteousness."

If the reader can follow us at this point, in the use of our own language, which language we have adopted after comparing our English version with the Greek version of the LXX, and the original Hebrew, grasping the whole question, at least, so far as represented in our Chart, and arranging our definitions upon this classification as a basis, our cherished hope is that we shall be able to make such a statement as to the relations of the Jewish Church to the Jewish nation and to other nations, or the relations of "the people of the congregation" to "the people of the land" and to "the peoples of the lands," as shall go far toward settling certain questions of present controversy, conceived to be highly important to the best interests of the Church and the world. *We ask the reader's careful attention!*

Tradition says that there were " two sorts of proselytes:" (1) *" the proselyte of the gate" or "proselyte of habitation," which were uncircumcised," and* (2), *the "proselytes of righteousness," which were circumcised and ate the passover."*

We say there were two sorts of landborns: (1) *the landborn in the gate or the landborn and dweller (resident landborn) which were uncircumcised, and* (2) *the landborns born again which were circumcised and ate the passover.*

I. The " landborn in the gates" and " landborn and dweller" (resident landborns).

We endeavored to point out in the previous chap-

ter, by what terms foreigners within "the commonwealth of Israel" were designated, viz.: The sons of outland, peoples of the lands, dwellers (resident foreigners), and nations ("Gentiles"). Any person so designated was a foreigner among "the people of the land," or within the Jewish nation, an alien among citizens, and a "stranger from the covenants of promise"—not to be circumcised nor allowed to eat the passover—but the children of a son of outland, or those "descended of a son of outland" (Gen. xvii, 12), or the "children of the dwellers" (resident foreigners) "and of their families which they begat in your land" (Lev. xxv, 45), were not sons of outland or foreign born, and were not necessarily reckoned with their parents as "aliens in the commonwealth of Israel and strangers from the covenants of promise." Such children being born in the land, had a choice of nationality, and, upon making this choice, were to be permitted to hold a covenant relation—to be circumcised. We now quote tradition, as given in *Cruden's Concordance* and the *Encyclopedia of Religious Knowledge*, article *Proselyte*, the reader remembering that the language quoted refers to a class of persons which we designate as "landborn in the gates" and "landborn and dweller" (resident landborns). A prerequisite with them to naturalization was, that the person *must be born in the land*, and, as we have just said, such had a choice of nationality, and when they "*would enter*

themselves as a landborn in the gates, or as a resident landborn, they promised with an oath in the presence of three witnesses, to keep those seven (ten commandments, as we have shown) precepts." "Their privileges were said to be: *First*, that by the observation of the rules of natural justice, and by exemption from idolatry, blasphemy, incest, adultery and murder (substantially the ten commandments), they thought they were in the path to eternal life" (in becoming one of the Jewish nation, the way to eternal life was now open to them, as the Rabbins taught that none but those of *their nation* would be saved). " *Secondly*, they might dwell in the land of Israel and share in the outward prosperities of the people of God." The expression, "outward prosperities," evidently alludes to the "tithes" of the fields which they now received every third year, and the privilege of "gleaning," which was now their right, and to the fact that they now became citizens of "the commonwealth" or "people of the land," who, as we have shown by actual reference, were under obligations to keep the ten commandments and to join in executing its penalties upon any offender. The landborn children of the sons of outland *entered themselves as a landborn in "the gates,"* or became one of "the people of the land" and assumed the obligations of one of "the people of the land" *by this oath—did not become a "proselyte" by this oath.* The parent was a son of outland, or a foreign-

er by birth, the child was a landborn; the parent was of the nations, the child was of *the nation*—became so in consequence of birth in the land, and an oath binding himself to perform all the duties of a citizen of the commonwealth, or one of "the people of the land," in whose name all civil matters were transacted (see Chart, section II).

II. *The landborn born again* ("proselytes of righteousness"). The born in the land, having become one of "the people of the land" in consequence of the birth and oath, as just referred to, could become one of "the people of the congregation," "congregation of the Lord," or landborn born again, in consequence of having, in the language of tradition, "*received, as it were, a new birth*" (being a landborn "born from above"—one "begat in your land," "begotten again unto a lively hope") and of having taken an oath (the oath of the covenant, the token of which "covenant of circumcision" he received "in his flesh") binding him to perform all the duties of the landborn born again, or one of "the people of the congregation," and live with them as those "whose praise is not of men but of God." The ordinance they received (circumcision) in becoming one of "the people of the congregation," has this meaning ("neither is that circumcision which is outward in the flesh," "we are the circumcision—*the regenerate*—which worship God in the spirit and rejoice in Christ Jesus, and have no confidence in the flesh,"

see Rom. ii, 28, 29; Phil. iii, 3); and in receiving it, they bound themselves to perform the duties of one of God's covenant people; and, performing those duties, were entitled to "covenant promises"—admission into that kingdom which, "except a man be born again, he can not see."

But more definitely. The Jewish Church (or "the people of the congregation"), from the very nature of its organization, received additions to its membership, only in two ways, viz.:

1. *Families of " the people of the land," or landborns, upon being born again and circumcised, " drew near" (entered among the "drawing nigh"—became members of the Jewish Church, or a family of " the people of the congregation") and ate the passover with the Hebrew of the Hebrews, and were thenceforth under the same laws (the laws by which " the people of the congregation" were governed) and were reckoned as a family of the tribe in whose bonds they professed conversion, and received an inheritance within that tribe.* "And when a landborn (one of "the people of the land") shall be born again with thee, and keep the passover to the Lord, let all his males (*an entire family*) be circumcised, and then let him come near and keep it; and he shall be as the Hebrew of the Hebrews of the land: for no uncircumcised (landborn) shall eat thereof. One law shall be to ("the people of the congregation") the Hebrew of the Hebrews and to the landborn born again among you" (Ex. xii, 48, 49). "So

shall ye divide this land unto you according to *the tribes* of Israel. And it shall come to pass, that ye shall divide it by lot for an *inheritance unto you*, and to the landborns born again among you, which shall beget children among you; and they shall be unto you as the Hebrew of the Hebrews among the children of Israel; they shall *have inheritance* with you among the tribes of Israel. And it shall come to pass, in what tribe the landborn is born again, *there shall ye give him his inheritance* saith the Lord God (Ez. xlvii, 21–23). *An entire family of landborns upon being born again and circumcised, ate the passover, and were thenceforth reckoned of " the people of the congregation" and a family of the tribe in whose midst they professed conversion, and as such, received an inheritance within the inheritance of that tribe.*

2. *An individual of a family of " the people of the land," or a landborn child of a son of outland, or one of " the children of the dwellers" (resident foreigners), or one of the children " of their families which they begat in your land"* (Lev. xxv, 45), *upon being born again and circumcised ("forsaking father and mother," and in receiving this ordinance, " received, as it were, a new birth"* —tradition) *became one of ("when thou hast circumcised him"*—Ex. xii, 44) *" the people of the congregation," in being incorporated in a family of the Hebrew of the Hebrews, or in a family of the landborn born again, as an adopted child and an heir, and received, with other children, an inheritance within the inheritance of the family*

—*received within the "heritage of God," or his Church, "an inheritance among them that are sanctified."*

The person to whom I refer in the above, is one of a class of persons often referred to in the Bible as belonging to households within the covenant of circumcision, and partakers of every privilege, but not "born in the house." They were children of a "household of God," in order to their becoming which, they "must needs be" "in the Lord" ("must needs be circumcised" as well as "the born in the house"—Gen. xvii, 13); but not children by natural birth. They are designated in our translation, by the expressions, "bought for money," or "bondmen that ye buy," and designated in tradition, as "proselytes of righteousness" or "proselytes of justice," and whom I designate as *the landborn born again*.

I now quote tradition, as given in the *Encyclopedia of Religious Knowledge*, in reference to the so-called "proselytes of justice or righteousness," the reader remembering that the language of the Rabbins refers to "*the landborn born again*," and observing that they are speaking *entirely of individuals*. "The landborn born again were those converted (converts) to Judaism, who had engaged themselves to receive circumcision, and to observe the whole law of Moses." "Thus they were admitted to all the prerogatives of the "*people of the Lord*" (one of "the people of the land" upon being born again and circumcised became one of "the people of the congregation").

"The Rabbins inform us, that before circumcision was administered to them, and before they were admitted into the religion of the Hebrews (into the Hebrew Church, or reckoned among 'the people of the congregation') they were examined about the motives to their conversion (the motives which determined them to seek to make a profession) whether the change was voluntary, or whether it proceeded from *interest* (the landborn upon being born again and circumcised received *an inheritance*), fear, ambition, etc." (it appearing that they were actuated by such motives, of course, they were rejected). "When the landborn was well proved and instructed (giving proper reasons for supposing he had experienced a change of heart—had been born again) they gave him circumcision (an ordinance which means regeneration), and when the wound of his circumcision healed, they gave him baptism, by plunging his whole body into a cistern of water by only one immersion." "Boys under twelve years of age and girls under thirteen, could not become *proselytes* (not be encouraged to forsake father and mother until years of discretion) till they had obtained the consent of their parents, or, in case of refusal, the concurrence of the officers of justice." "Baptism*

---

* So far as I have observed, I have seen no intimation in tradition that there was a "baptism" or any "washing" connected with becoming a "proselyte of the gate" or "proselyte of habitation;" that is, any "baptism" or "washings" connected with the forms

in respect of girls had the same effect as circumcision in respect of boys. Each of them by means of this received as it were, a new birth (born "into the

---

by which one born in the land came to be reckoned a "landborn in the gate" or "landborn and dweller" (resident landborn), or one of "the people of the land." "Proselyte baptism," or that "baptism" which a landborn upon being born again, is said to have received as part of the "ceremony," by which he was transferred to a family of "the people of the congregation," is a thing entirely of tradition. There were "washings" connected with the restoration to the congregation of members of the congregation separated for an offense or as unclean, often referred to in the Bible —"shall both wash his clothes and bathe himself in water and be *unclean* until the even: then shall he be *clean*"—and it is indeed probable that these same "washings" were practiced in the reception of a person for the first time among "the people of the congregation;" since in this reception a person *unclean* became *clean*. So far as the controversy of modern time about "baptism" is stated in the following extract from an article "prepared expressly" for the *Encyclopedia of Religious Knowledge*, by a baptist, Rev. James D. Knowles, Professor in the Newton Theological Institute, our work will throw much light upon the issues made. We quote: "Among the other ways by which the practice (infant baptism) is defended, the only one which can now be alluded to, and the one on which the greatest stress has been laid, is, that the covenant with Abraham was a spiritual covenant, and that as such, it included infants; that they were accordingly circumcised under the old dispensation; that baptism is a substitute for circumcision, and that consequently infants are to be baptized. The Baptists deny the truth of every part of this argument. They deny that there was any such thing as a Church among the Jews; that is, a separate body of true saints. The whole nation was considered as one political body, and the rite of circumcision was a national mark of

kingdom of God"—"by this means" one of "the people of the land" became one of "the people of the congregation"), so that those who were their parents before were no longer regarded as such after this ceremony."

I have endeavored to direct the attention of the reader to the true meaning of the above tradition, by inclosing remarks in parentheses, it having been shown in the foregoing Chart that the ancient *prosēlutoi* of either class, concerning whom the Rabbins are evidently talking, were not sons of outland or converted foreigners. In the light of the above tradition and our own analysis, it would appear that any person of mature years, a landborn child either of a family of "the people of the land," or "the peoples of the lands," upon passing an approved examination, in the reception of the ordinance of circumcision, received, as it were, a new birth," and "those who were their parents before were no longer

---

distinction which all male Jews, whether pious or wicked, were required to possess. Male infants were accordingly circumcised, not because their parents were pious, but because they were Jews; and the Jews were required to circumcise their male servants, whether born in their houses, or bought with their money, on precisely the same principle that they circumcised their children, viz.: because those servants and children were now members of the Jewish nation." The reader of this work will hardly need the remark here, that "the people of the land" was *the nation;* and "the people of the congregation" was that "separate body of true saints," called "*the Church.*"

regarded as such after this ceremony" (being received—"when thou hast circumcised him"—Ex. xii, 44—*as children* of "parents," the heads of a family of "the people of the congregation").

It is very obvious, that no child whose parents were of "the people of the land" (much less the landborn child whose parents "were foreigners," "Gentiles," or "peoples of the lands"), could remain connected with such a family, and yet become a child of "the covenant of circumcision." The profession referred to above, involved "the forsaking father and mother" for a home within "the kingdom of God" on earth in a household of "the people of the congregation." Such an idea as a child of the covenant, or one of "the people of the congregation" living in a family and under the direction of the head of a family of "the people of the land," even though the master or ruler of that household was a most worthy man as a citizen of "the commonwealth of Israel," is entirely at variance with the whole spirit of that economy. Baptism, administered by one not a member of any Church, would not be recognized as valid baptism by any body of Christians of our day; so, under the former economy, the seal of the covenant was administered by those within the covenant of circumcision. We read of those introduced into families of "the people of the congregation," by the reception of the ordinance of circumcision ("when thou hast cir-

cumcised him"—Ex. xii, 44), and have repeatedly shown that they were landborns, and that the ordinance they received (circumcision) signifies to be born again; or, in the language of tradition, in the reception of this ordinance, "they received, as it were, *a new birth*," and "those who were their parents before were no longer regarded as such after this ceremony."

This convert in a family of "the people of the congregation" was a son and heir in the house of his spiritual father, and, like all other children of the household, was a servant, or one under the government and instruction of that "master of Israel" into whose household he had been admitted upon being "born again" and circumcised, and in which admission he had entered into "the kingdom of God" upon earth; and, being "faithful unto death," held the Divine promise, "the oath of the covenant," that he should be admitted into "the kingdom of God" on high—"ye which have followed me *in the regeneration*, when the Son of man shall sit in the throne of his glory, ye shall also sit upon twelve thrones, judging the twelve tribes of Israel. *And every one that hath forsaken houses, or brethren or sisters, or father or mother, or wife or children, or lands for my name's sake, shall receive an hundredfold, and shall inherit* (inheriting in the earthly was an assurance or pledge of a title to an "inheritance" in the heavenly Canaan) *everlasting life*" (Matt. xix, 28, 29).

We remark again, before proceeding further, that the Rabbins, in the tradition given above, can not possibly refer to what we have referred to under the previous head, respecting *an entire family* of "the people of the land," upon being born again and circumcised, becoming a family of "the people of the congregation," as in Ex. xii, 48. *This tradition alludes to individuals*—"to boys and girls," and to their examination "about the motives to their conversion" " before they were admitted into the religion of the Hebrews" (the Jewish Church), and these "boys and girls"—if under a certain age upon conditions, if over that age without conditions—might " forsake father and mother" (separate themselves from their father's house) " so that those who were their parents before were no longer regarded as such after this ceremony " (circumcision and baptism). In Ex. xii, 48, the entire family were converted and drew near and kept the passover to the Lord as a family, the heads of the house and the children continuing in their proper relations as parents and children, and all were thus admitted among "the people of the congregation," and kept the passover as a family; *so that the above tradition can not possibly refer to the additions made to the Hebrew Church, as authorized in* Ex. xii, 48.

This is further evident when we observe, that, *impliedly, the heads of another family were* " regarded as their parents after this ceremony." Such a trans-

for, only after an examination, in which the candidate must give proper evidence of fitness for the position sought, *presupposes* a home and a father's house about to be enjoyed more desirable in a religious point of view, and, if by "consent of (ungodly) parents," certainly not less desirable in a temporal point of view; but whether by "consent of the parents," or choice of the child independent of the parents, the new relation was one desired and earnestly *sought by the child at least.* This tradition evidently relates to something very different from that referred to in Ex. xii, 48. But "*they received, as it were, a new birth.*" Will the reader refer me to a single passage, in our English translation, giving the remotest allusion to any one of the above items of Rabbinical tradition? Prominent writers will assert that the doctrine of the "new birth" is a doctrine peculiar to the New Testament Church; as though the Saviour, in the language, "Art thou a master of Israel and knowest not" that "except a man be born again he can not see the kingdom of God?" rebuked Nicodemus for not knowing what the Bible never taught him! If these writers are correct, unless Abraham and Isaac and Jacob experienced this "new birth" unwittingly, it is a vain hope that "many from the east and from the west" indulge of "sitting down with Abraham and Isaac and Jacob in the kingdom of heaven;" for if these "worthies" were not "born again," according to

the Saviour's language, they never saw that "kingdom," are not now sitting in it, and we shall never sit with them in that kingdom! Now, it is utterly inconceivable that the Church, under the old economy, received persons as individuals into membership, after the manner so fully set forth in the above tradition, without being able to refer to one passage of Scripture authorizing such additions.

The details of the above tradition are truly valuable, in the present circumstances of the case—*thanks to an all-wise Providence*—but this tradition is not necessary to the clear understanding of the whole question. The Divine word, when understood as it may and ought to be, is all sufficient for our understanding of every essential particular as given in the above tradition. The ordinance received (meaning to be born again—" neither is that circumcision which is outward in the flesh "), and the person receiving it (the landborn) are suggestive. The nature of the covenant engagements which the person assumed, in receiving the token of the covenant in his flesh, presupposes a person of years of discretion and clear understanding on his part of the duties and responsibilities of his new position—a clear understanding of the duties required and the hopes and promises of the covenant, and also a clear understanding of the consequences of a neglect of duty—" suspension " or " excommunication." The kingdom into which the person was introduced

"when thou hast circumcised him." (Ex. xii, 44), requires us to suppose the person willing to forsake "father and mother," if necessary to his admittance into this kingdom; which in this case was necessary, inasmuch as the parents, being foreigners, might not enter this kingdom. The very terms of the covenant, which were embodied subsequently in the law, make plain much that is not even referred to in the above tradition. Thus, "any son of outland shall not eat of it" (the passover—Ex. xii, 43); and as circumcision was the ordinance of introduction into the congregation and to the observance of the passover, of course a son of outland might not be circumcised. Hence the covenant as given to Abraham required that the "born in the house" and those " descended of any son of outland" "shall be circumcised" (Gen. xvii, 12), and (13), these two classes "must needs be circumcised," and on "the self same day" in which the covenant was given, "every male among the men of Abraham's house," the "born in the house," and " the descended of and separated from a son of outland, were circumcised with him" (Gen. xvii, 23, 27). The "descended of a son of outland" was a landborn, and that landborn, separating himself from his father's house and all foreign associations, after an examination according to the nature of the engagement about to be assumed, "when thou hast circumcised him" (Ex. xii, 44) became a landborn born again—became a

child of the covenant of circumcision in a "house" in which he was "not born," and enjoyed every privilege of "the born in the house" in that family of "the people of the congregation." *Thus it may be seen that the essentials of the above tradition are either given in, or plainly inferable from, the Divine word itself.*

We have given, on page 51, right hand column, the only possible renderings (see also pages 101–104) which can be made of Gen. xvii, 12 ; Gen. xvii, 27; Lev. xxv, 44, 45, so that these passages shall not contradict the plain declarations of the Scriptures in Ex. xii, 43; Neh. ix, 2; Ezra ix, 1; Lam. i, 10, and Ex. xii, 45 (compare pages 51 and 52, right hand column). These passages of Scripture, as we have explained them, are consistent, as the reader may see by reference to these explanations, which we need not here repeat; but we will refer to one of them (Lev. xxv, 45) to illustrate further our positions in the light of the above tradition and our own explanations: "Moreover, of the children of the dwellers (resident foreigners) *that do act the ger* among you," "and (of the children) of their families that are with you which *they begat in your land.*" We read, Ex. xii, 48, "And when a ger will act the ger, or a landborn shall be born again, or one begotten in your land shall be 'begotten again unto a lively hope,' and will keep the passover to the Lord, let all his males be circumcised and then let him come near and keep it;" so here we read, when the

children of the dwellers (resident foreigners) *shall act the ger* among you, or when the children of the dwellers (resident foreigners) shall be born again " among you " " and (the children) of their families that are with you, which they begat in your land " are " begotten again unto a lively hope " (the equivalent of the expression, " born again ") and " will keep the passover to the Lord," " when thou hast circumcised (a " hope " expressed entitled him to the ordinance) him then shall he eat thereof" (Ex. xii, 44). *I repeat:* The landborn children of resident foreigners (the " alien " or those of the uncircumcision, such as Ittai the Gittite) and (the children) of their families which they begat in your land—a son over twelve or a daughter over thirteen years of age—upon being born again (upon professing conversion) after " they were examined about the motives to their conversion, whether the change was voluntary, or whether it proceeded from interest, fear, ambition, etc.," upon " being well proved and instructed, were circumcised and baptized," (each of them " by this means receiving, *as it were, a new birth*"); and were said henceforth "to be born again," or " regenerate," and by the reception of these ordinances (circumcision and baptism) representative of this fact, and accepted as a fact by those in authority, upon such evidence as that referred to above, were transferred, or, as it were, circumcised and baptized into a new household—in a particular case,

transferred from the household of Ittai, an "alien and stranger from the covenants," to a household within the covenant of circumcision; or, as correctly expressed in the above tradition, so far as that tradition goes, "so that those who were their parents before were no longer regarded as such after this ceremony."

Who were regarded as their parents after this ceremony? "And ye shall take them as an inheritance for your children after you, to inherit them for a possession" (Lev. xxv, 46). Shall we say that the landborn children of an alien family, or of a family of the uncircumcision, upon such a profession, after such an examination, were transferred from the family of the "alien," if under twelve or thirteen years of age, only by consent of the "alien" parents or the judges, to a membership in a spiritual household within the covenant, upon such evidences of a spiritual birth, and were *regarded henceforth in that household as adopted children and heirs?* When we understand who they were, their character, the nature of the transfer, the meaning of Lev. xxv, 46, is plain— *And ye yourselves (hithpael) shall make them inherit among your children after you unto the inheriting (that they may inherit) a possession*—that is, "*an inheritance* (in the earthly Canaan) *among them that are sanctified*" (*i.e.*, among the Hebrew of the Hebrews, or the landborn born again), Acts xxvi, 18. "And if *children,* then *heirs;* heirs of God (in the "heritage

of God ") and joint heirs of (the elder brother, the type of) Christ" (Rom. viii, 17). "Thus were they admitted to all the prerogatives of the people of the Lord" (tradition)—"people of the congregation." Then "they were admitted into the congregation of the Lord as adopted children" (Dr. Tomline). Not only "*so that those who were their parents before were no longer regarded as such after this ceremony*," but thenceforth they were "considered" as children—"reckoned for the seed"—in that pious household within the covenant into which they were introduced by this "new birth" as children. Born in the land and born again, "forsaking father and mother," and solemnly dedicating themselves to God in a covenant, the token of which covenant they received in their flesh, were they not ("*worthy of me*") worthy to be children in the household of the covenant into which, being born in the land, it was their privilege *to be "adopted"* ("my kinsman according to the flesh," "to whom pertaineth the *adoption*, and the glory, and the covenants," etc., Rom. ix, 34), and were such not "worthy"—"meet"—to have in that land "*an inheritance* among them that are sanctified" and "meet to be partakers of *the inheritance* of the saints in light?"

Such were *children and heirs in the earthly Canaan*, and such, "faithful unto death," held a title under "the oath of promise" to an inheritance in the heavenly Canaan—such had the assurance of the

oath of God that ere long they should be ushered as "children" and "heirs" into that "house not made with hands eternal in the heavens." *Then, individuals, landborns, the children of a son of outland, or the children of dwellers (resident foreigners), or the children of " their families that are with you which they begat in your land" upon being " begotten again" or " born again" after such an examination as referred to above by the Rabbins (after an examination according to the nature of the covenant engagement about to be assumed, " when thou hast circumcised him "*—Ex. xii, 44), *in the reception of this ordinance " received, as it were, a new birth" and became children of the covenant of circumcision in a " house" in which they were " not born," and enjoyed every privilege with other children in that family of " the people of the congregation"—eating the passover and receiving an inheritance within the inheritance of the family.*

All this, indeed, may be told very briefly: "Any son of outland" (Ex. xii, 43) and "any uncircumcised (unregenerate) landborn shall not eat of it" (the passover—Ex. xii, 48). *An entire family* of landborns upon being born again and circumcised were added to, and thenceforth reckoned as *a family* of "the people of the congregation" of a certain tribe; *an individual*, a landborn, upon being born again and circumcised was added to, and thenceforth reckoned as *a member of a family* of "the people of the congregation" of a certain tribe; the family receiving an inheritance within the inherit-

ance of the tribe, the individual receiving an inheritance within the inheritance of the family, to which each respectively was added on the reception of the ordinance of circumcision; and, whether previous to or not, at least at the jubilee, every male of the above classes of landborns born again, having a wife and children, became a "master of Israel," or the head of a family of "the people of the congregation," and received an inheritance in the reallotment of the jubilee—"ye shall divide it by lot for an inheritance *unto you, and to the landborns born again among you, which shall beget children among you;* and they shall be unto you as the Hebrew of the Hebrews (as the "clean") among the children of Israel, they shall have inheritance with you among the tribes of Israel. And it shall come to pass in what tribe the landborn is born again, there shall ye give him his inheritance, saith the Lord God" (Ez. xlvii, 22, 23).

This, as I understand it, is the substance of "the ordinance of the passover," or the law by which "the people of the congregation" were to be governed in the admission of families and individuals to their number, and the privileges to which these families and individuals were entitled when thus admitted to the "kingdom of God" upon earth. I have heretofore referred to the fact, found in the discipline of the Jewish Church, that offenders among "the people of the congregation" were liable

to "*suspension*" and "*excommunication*" (to be held "as a heathen man"), while the death penalty was an act of "the people of the land" or civil Israel, upon any offender against the civil law within the limits of the nation.

I. I observe, that there was as much regularity in the organization of the Church under that economy as in any branch of the New Testament Church of our own time. Thus a family of landborns was added to a tribe and was one of a number of families which made up that tribe; and an individual landborn was added to a family, and was one of a number of individuals who made up that family; so a church is added to a presbytery and is one of a number of churches which make up that presbytery, and an individual is added to a church and is one of a number of individuals who make up that church.

II. The office of a "master of Israel," or the office of the head of a household of "the people of the congregation," and the office of the "gospel minister" or "pastor of a church," are substantially the same office, as may be seen from a glance at the nature of the duties of each, and the reward promised to those faithful in the discharge of these duties.

(1) According to the language of the Saviour to Nicodemus, it was expected that a "master of Israel" should know, and of course teach, "Except a

man be born again he can not see the kingdom of God." The "master of Israel" taught, and the "gospel minister" must teach, "ye must be born again."

(2) The "master of Israel" administered, and the "gospel minister" administers, the ordinance of admission into the Church. The "gospel minister," being satisfied, "after an examination about the motives to a conversion," that a soul is regenerate (is born again), administers to that person the ordinance of baptism, and that person is received into the Church of God, sits down at the table of the Lord, and is thenceforth reckoned in "the kingdom of God," having a "right to all the privileges of the sons of God." The "master of Israel," or the head of a "household of God," upon being satisfied, "after an examination about the motives to their conversion" (tradition), that the landborn child of a son of outland, or one of "the children of the dwellers" (resident foreigners), or one of the children of "their families which they begat in your land," was "born again," or "begotten again unto a lively (living) hope," administered the ordinance of circumcision, and the person was received into a "household of God" and took a seat among the "born in the house," at the passover table ("when thou hast circumcised him then shall he eat thereof," Ex. xii, 44) and was thenceforth reckoned within "the kingdom of God," having a "right to all the privileges of the

sons of God"—"eating bread" in "the kingdom" and receiving "an inheritance (in the earthly Canaan) among them that are sanctified."

(3) The "master of Israel" not only taught as the "gospel minister" now teaches, "ye must be born again;" and not only administered the ordinance of admission into the Church, upon proper evidence being given that a soul was regenerate, as the "gospel minister" now administers such an ordinance upon the same evidence; but the duties of the "master of Israel," under the Old Testament economy, as an under-shepherd of "the great shepherd of Israel" having oversight of the flock, "the regenerate," "the heritage of God" or the Church, were the same duties as those of the gospel minister now are in the same charge; and to the faithful under-shepherd then, as now, there were promises of a glorious reward.

What these duties are, the Divine master himself, "the captain of the Lord's host" (Josh. v, 15), "the captain of their salvation" (Heb. ii, 10), the great "shepherd of Israel that leadeth Joseph like a flock" (Ps. lxxx, 1), and the leader of his "Church in the wilderness" ("if thy presence go not with me, carry us not up hence," Ex. xxxiii, 15), set forth, while upon earth, *both by precept and example.* "One is *your master*, even Christ; and all *ye are brethren*," and "If I then, your Lord and master, have washed your feet; ye also ought to wash one

another's feet; for I have given you an example" —an "ensample for the flock." In *this kingdom,* " Whosoever will be great among you, let him be your minister; and whosoever will be chief among you, let him be your servant: even as the son of man came not to be ministered unto, but to minister, and to give his life a ransom for many." Let " the princes of the Gentiles exercise dominion (domineer) over them, and they that are great exercise authority (lord it) upon them," if they choose so to do, " but it shall not be so among you "— shall not *be so in this kingdom. These are the duties of an under-shepherd as laid down by " the chief-shepherd," the great " master" himself.*

The apostle Peter lays down the duties and hopes of the "gospel minister" or of an under-shepherd, in language not to be mistaken, " Feed the flock of God which is among you, taking the oversight thereof, not by constraint, but willingly; not for filthy lucre, but of a ready mind; neither as being lords (domineering) over God's heritage, but being ensamples (as Christ the master set an example) for the flock. And (your reward shall be), when the chief-shepherd shall appear, ye shall receive a crown of glory that fadeth not away" (1 Pet. v, 2–4). Such are the duties and the hopes of an under-shepherd, or a "gospel minister," in charge of the " flock of God," " the regenerate," " the heritage of

God," or the Church of God, in New Testament times.

The apostle alludes, in the expression, "heritage of God," to that body of people, in Old Testament times, to whom "God gave (Ps. cxxxv, 12) the land of Canaan for a heritage" (the regenerate or born again, as we have seen)—to that body of people whose sins are pardoned, "Who is a God like unto thee, that pardoneth iniquity, and passeth by the transgression of the remnant of *his heritage* (Micah vii, 18) ?—" the heritage of God," "the flock of God," "the regenerate," or the Church of God.

The charge of the apostle, as given above, is but a repetition of the charge given by the great "shepherd of Israel," to his under-shepherds in charge of "the heritage of God," or "the regenerate," before as yet the chief shepherd had become incarnate and given his life for the flock. In the same verse in which it is enjoined upon a "master of Israel" to receive the landborn, upon being born again and circumcised, as a child and an heir; or in the same verse in which it is commanded that a landborn, "following" an under-shepherd "in the regeneration" shall receive an inheritance in the earthly Canaan; or, changing the figure again, in the same verse, in which it is commanded that "the adoption" shall receive "an inheritance among them that are sanctified" in the earthly Canaan, the duties of a "master of Israel," or of an under-shep-

herd, in charge of the "heritage of God," under that economy, are laid down, in language substantially the same as that used by the chief shepherd while upon earth, or as that used by the apostle Peter, " *over your brethren the children of Israel, ye shall not rule ('domineer' or be as 'lords over God's heritage') one (Israelite) over another (one become an Israelite in being adopted into your household) with rigor*" (Lev. xxv, 46). "Ye," "masters of Israel," "under-shepherds," the heads of households of "the people of the congregation," or "households of God," *beware how you exercise authority* over "the children of dwellers (resident foreigners) who do act the ger, or are born again with you;" and *beware how you exercise authority* over the children "of their families that are with you which they begat in your land," who, having "forsaken father and mother," have been united to your household as a "household of God" in the reception of an ordinance by which they were received and acknowledged as the land-born born again or "the regenerate;" and *beware how you exercise authority, how you lord it* over "your brethren the children of Israel," over the "heritage of God," if you would "receive a crown of glory that fadeth not away when the chief shepherd shall appear." *This is that counsel which the great "shepherd of Israel" gave his under-shepherds, from the beginning, and which he repeated to his twelve apostles while upon earth; and which these apostles enjoined upon those under-*

shepherds having charge of the "flock of God" in New Testament times.

The duties, then, of a "master of Israel," were substantially the same as the duties of a "gospel minister." Each under their respective economies were to teach (1), the same doctrine—the doctrine of regeneration; (2), administer to the regenerate the ordinance of admission into the Church; and (3), each were to have oversight of "the regenerate," the "flock of God," the "heritage of God" or the Church of God.

But, had the "masters of Israel" an assurance, with gospel ministers, that, *not* "being lords over God's heritage, but being ensamples for the flock," " when the chief shepherd shall appear" they should " receive a crown of glory that fadeth not away "— had the " *master of Israel*" *an assurance or promise of eternal life?* The land belonging to the Lord ("the land shall *not be sold forever;* for the land is mine" Lev. xxv, 23—" a dwelling-house in a walled city " " shall be *established forever to him that bought it throughout his generations; it shall not go out in the jubilee,"* Lev. xxv, 29, 30), the " master of Israel " "freely having received (an inheritance in the reallotment of the jubilee) freely gave" (shared that inheritance with " the adoption "). " Freely ye (gospel minister) have received (a title to eternal life) freely give" (freely share with your spiritual children that which you have received of God as a gift of his

grace). The under-shepherd must imitate the example of the chief-shepherd in dispensing freely spiritual blessings. There can be no mistake *as to the meaning of this free gift of God to the regenerate, of an inheritance in the earthly Canaan.* It was a gift by which he pledged himself to those who were "faithful unto death," that they should receive " an inheritance incorruptible, undefiled, and that fadeth not away." This earthly home, the gift of God's grace to them, like all earthly things, might fade away, but not so " the mansion" which it represented in " the skies" —that "house not made with hands, eternal in the heavens." The possessing, by divine appointment, " an inheritance among them that are sanctified" in the earthly Canaan, seems to have been a foretaste or pledge to such of "an inheritance among them that are sanctified" in the heavenly Canaan. The patriarchs " desired a better country, that is, a heavenly "—" looked for a city, which hath foundations, whose builder and maker is God" (Heb. xi, 10). This is no new doctrine, and there can be no mistake as to the hope which a " master of Israel" was entitled to entertain; and there can be no mistake as to the hope which a landborn " forsaking father and mother" and following a " master of Israel," or an under-shepherd in " the regeneration" was entitled to entertain. They had not only the promises of the covenant of circumcision, but hope was shadowed forth to them in that they, in being intro-

duced among the regenerate, were made heirs, and, in due time, they, as members of a "household of God," were put in possession of "an inheritance among them that are sanctified" in the earthly Canaan—"a pattern of things in the heavens" (Heb. ix, 23), and to them "a shadow of good things to come." A "shadow" to them (the regenerate) of a home in the "household of God," in that "house not made with hands, eternal in the heavens," and a "pattern of things in the heavens," in that the regenerate only shall inherit the kingdom of God on high. At the last day the king shall say, "Come, ye blessed of my father, inherit the kingdom prepared for you from the foundation of the world;" that is, the regenerate only are "blessed" and brought into possession of this inheritance; for, "Except a man be born again, he can not see the kingdom of God."

Allusions to "the adoption," and to the ground of assurance which they had of eternal life, under the Old Testament economy, abound in the New Testament Scriptures. The expressions, "shall inherit eternal life," "shall inherit everlasting life," "shall inherit the kingdom of God," "partakers of the inheritance of the saints in light," refer to assurances which "the heritage of God," "the regeneration," "the sanctified," "the adoption," "the righteous," and "households of God" have had from the beginning. "And now brethren, I com-

mend you to God, and to the word of his grace, which is able to build you up, and to give *you an inheritance among all them that* are sanctified (Acts xx, 32). Not only among those who had been sanctified and saved during the few years which the New Testament economy had existed, but among all those who, from the beginning, had been sanctified and entered into " the inheritance of the saints in light." " The righteous," in Solomon's time, " had hope in his death." The apostle alludes, in the following, to the landborn born again, as adopted into a " household of God;" that is, " the adoption," or " the regeneration," and to their hopes. "And if children (in a ' household of God') then heirs (in ' the heritage' or Church) of God, and joint heirs with Christ (the chief-shepherd), if so be that we suffer (' faithful unto death ') with him, that we may be also glorified together" (Rom. viii, 17). A landborn, " forsaking father and mother," upon giving satisfactory evidence of a new birth, in being circumcised, was received as a *child* (" those who were his parents before being no longer regarded as such after this ceremony"—tradition) in a " household of God," and the apostle draws *the sequence:* "And if children, then heirs," etc.—sharing with a "master of Israel," or an under-shepherd, as heir or " joint heir," an inheritance in the earthly Canaan and—" saved in hope"—prospectively sharing with the chief shepherd an inheritance in the heavenly

Canaan, if he continued faithful, "if so be that we suffer," etc.

The exact state of things as they existed in the Church or "heritage of God," the special charge of the "chief-shepherd," and sanctifier of the "people of the congregation" (*khahal*, Heb.—*ecclesia*, Sept.), under the former economy, is referred to in the Epistle to the Hebrews: "For it became him (God the Father) for whom are all things, and by whom are all things, in bringing many *sons* unto glory, to make the captain of their salvation perfect through sufferings. For both he that sanctifieth and they who are sanctified are all of one; for which cause he is not ashamed to call them brethren, saying, I will declare thy name unto my brethren; in the midst of the Church (Greek, *ecclesia*) will I sing praise unto thee. And again, I will put my trust in him. And again, Behold I and the children which God hath given me" (Heb. ii, 10–13).

(1) The "adoption," or the landborn born again, in a household of the "people of the congregation" (*khahal*, Heb.—*ecclesia*, Sept.), a "household of God," were "sons" with those of that household, on their way to "glory"—"sons" and "heirs" of the gifts of God's grace, an inheritance in his kingdom on earth, and an inheritance in his kingdom on high.

(2) "The captain of the Lord's host" (Josh. v, 15), the "shepherd of Israel that leadeth Joseph

like a flock" (Ps. lxxx, 1), the leader of the "Church (*ecclesia*) in the wilderness" (Acts vii, 38), "the messenger of the covenant" and "my messenger" whom "I will send" (Malachi iii, 1), "Jesus Christ, the same yesterday and to-day and forever" (Heb. xiii, 8), *was "the captain of their salvation"* and the sanctifier of those "sons," who, "forsaking father and mother" for his sake, in the reception of "the token of the covenant" in their flesh, were received among "the clean" as children of the covenant and children of the head of a "household of God;" and, "sanctified and meet for the master's use," by command of "the sanctifier," or the "chief-shepherd," speaking in his word to an under-shepherd, they received "an inheritance" in the earthly Canaan as "children" and "heirs" in a "household of God"—"among them that are sanctified."

(3) The apostle says, that the "messenger of the covenant," the "sanctifier" of his people and "captain of their salvation," and the people which he sanctified were "one" people—"for both he that sanctifieth and they who are sanctified are all of one"—and therefore it is that, "speaking by the mouth of David," he called them *brethren*, saying, "I will declare thy name (the name of the father) unto *my brethren*, in the midst of the congregation (*khahal*, Heb.—*ecclesia*, Sept.) will I praise thee" (Ps. xxii, 22); and therefore it is that, he, by the mouth of the prophet Isaiah, calls them *children*,

saying, "Behold, I and *the children* whom the Lord hath given me" (Isa. viii, 18). I have repeatedly pointed out that the "people of the congregation" (*khahal*, Heb.—*ecclesia*, Sept.) were composed of households of the "Hebrew of the Hebrews," and households of the landborn born again. *It appears, therefore, that "the adoption," or the landborn born again, in a "household of God," were not only "children" and "brethren" of a "master of Israel," or an under-shepherd, over which "brethren of the children of Israel" this under-shepherd must "not rule with rigor"* (Lev. xxv, 46); *but they were "children" and "brethren" of the "chief-shepherd"—"sons" on their way to "glory,"sanctified by the "messenger of the covenant" and "the captain of their salvation," under that economy, and the captain of our salvation, "Jesus Christ, the same yesterday and to-day and forever!"*

Is there anything unseemly in saying, that every "child of the covenant" was a "brother" and "heir" with every other "child of the covenant," under Christ the master and "messenger of the covenant" under that economy? I take the position, that every true "shepherd of Israel" and those "following" him "in the regeneration"— that every "child of the covenant" had an assurance of everlasting life, confirmed by the most solemn promises and pledges; *and more*, the chief-shepherd, speaking by the prophet Isaiah, gave similar assurances to others, as well as those of that

"fold" within the Jewish nation. The sons of outland, "that kept the Sabbath from polluting it, and took hold of his covenant," he assured, that their prayers should be heard, that "their sacrifices should be accepted upon his altar," and that he would gather "others ('the outcasts of Israel,' 'strangers from the covenants of promise,' or pious foreigners) to him beside those that are gathered unto him" (Isa. lvi, 6–8)—that he would gather home to his fold, "the Jerusalem above the mother of *us all*," not only the pious Jew but the pious "Gentile," and "there shall be one fold and one shepherd." "In time past," or under the Hebrew economy, "the *xenoi* of the covenants of promise," or the *xenoi* and dwellers (resident foreigners), could not be "fellow-citizens with the saints and of the household of God" (Eph. ii, 11, 19)—could not be members of a household of "the people of the congregation" and of the fold of an under-shepherd, and therefore not of that particular fold of the chief-shepherd.

We have set forth the hopes which the "master of Israel" and those "following" him "in the regeneration"—the hopes which all the children of the covenant were entitled to entertain. The prominent stipulation of the covenant of circumcision was, that the person covenanting, in whatever sphere he might be called to act, engaged to be one "whose praise is not of men but of God" (Rom. ii, 29).

This high regard for God and his cause required the "master of Israel" to "love the landborn born again as himself" (Lev. xix, 34), and receive him into his household as a "child" and an "heir," giving him "an inheritance among them that are sanctified," while at the same time, duty to God, might require him to separate his own "mocking" Ishmael from his household, its duties and its privileges. On the other hand "the adoption" in a "household of God," was one who had "forsaken father and mother," and broken off every natural tie, that he might become a "child of the covenant" and be numbered among those "whose praise is not of men but of God." On the part of each, therefore, God's approval or "praise" was *the consideration*, with which any natural affection must not interfere. At the age of *twelve* the child (*pais*) Jesus was found "at the feast of the passover" "sitting in the midst of the doctors," and his language, "wist ye not that I must be about my father's business," implies that the age had come when his duty to God was paramount. A person of his age and sense of duty—a landborn, whose parents were foreigners, "his father's business" would have required to forsake father and mother for a home in a "household of the people of the congregation," into which, introduced in the reception of the ordinance of circumcision as a "child of the covenant," he now, in a

"household of God," would eat the passover "in a house" in which he was *not* "born."

The names, "thy bondmen" and "thy bondmaids" (Lev. xxv, 44), by which our translators designate the landborn born again, or "the adoption," in a "household of God," convey, of course, an erroneous impression. By the LXX, they are designated as *pais* and *paidiskea*. Take a sample of Greek usage: "unto you first God having raised up his son (*pais*) Jesus" (Acts iii, 26); *not bondman Jesus*—"against thy holy child (*pais*) Jesus... and that signs and wonders may be done by the name of thy holy child (*pais*) Jesus" (Acts iv, 27-30); *not holy bondman Jesus*—" master look upon my son (*uios*); for he is mine only child" (only begotten) ... Bring hither my son (*uios*). And as he was yet coming, the devil threw him down and tare him. And Jesus rebuked the unclean spirit and healed the child (*pais*) and delivered him again to his Father" (Luke ix, 38, 41, 42); *Father and son, not master and bondman or slave*—" Behold my servant (Sept., *pais*, son) whom I uphold; *mine elect (not my bondman!)* in whom my soul delighteth; I have put my spirit upon him; he shall bring forth judgment to the Gentiles" or nations (Isa. xlii, 1).

Following the LXX and this Greek usage—instances of which usage might be multiplied almost indefinitely—I read, Lev. xxv, 44: "Your servants and your handmaids," your young men and your

maidens, which were *your sons and your daughters*, "the adoption" in a "household of God." "Your" can not refer to the head of a household of "the people of the land," an uncircumcised household, but must refer to the shepherd and his flock. Abraham circumcised "the born in his house and the bought with money (*min-eth*), descended of and separated from a son of outland" (Gen. xvii, 27); so here, those young men and maidens which "thou shalt have" and of whom "ye shall buy," are those (*min-eth*) "descended of and separated from the nations round about" (Lev. xxv, 44); but "the bought with thy money must needs be circumcised" (Gen. xvii, 13), and "when thou hast circumcised him then shall he eat thereof" (the passover, Ex. xii, 44). Further; we know that the children of the dwellers (resident foreigners) who do act the ger with you—who were born again, or who "followed" a master of Israel in "the regeneration"—were of "the people of the congregation;" and we know just how "the children of their families that are with you, which they begat in your land" (Lev. xxv, 45) came to be "your children," "the adoption" or "the regeneration" in "your" households, viz.: in the reception of the ordinance of circumcision "they received, as it were, a *new birth* (such in 'your' household were 'the regeneration'), so that those who were their parents before were no longer regarded as such (such children in 'your' household

were 'the adoption' or 'your' children) after this ceremony" (tradition). And now, having "forsaken father and mother," and "followed" you "in the regeneration" * are your young men and maid-

---

* The form of Church organization called "the Church in the house" does not seem to have ceased immediately upon the abrogation of the Jewish economy. "At first, all who were engaged in propagating Christianity administered this rite; nor can it be called in question that whoever persuaded any person to embrace Christianity, could baptize his own disciple. But when the Churches became more regulated, and were provided with rules of order, the bishop alone exercised the right of baptizing all the new converts to Christianity." (See *Mosheim's Ecclesiastical History*, Book I, Century I, Part II, Chapter IV, Section 8). In the next Century, we read (see Book I, Part II, Chapter IV, Section 13): "Adults were to prepare their minds (for baptism) expressly, by prayers, fasting, and other devotional exercises. *Sponsors or godfathers* were, as I apprehend, first employed *for adults*, and afterward for children likewise."

The "master of Israel" only "discipled" and administered the ordinance of circumcision to such as were of his *own nation*, "people of the land," or the landborn children of foreign families. The commission of the gospel minister is *more extensive:* "Go ye therefore and teach (or disciple) *all nations*, baptizing them in the name of the Father, and of the Son, and of the Holy Ghost (Matt. xxviii, 19). The relation of the " godfather " (" father in God ") and the " adult " *in the second century;* and the relation of that *person* (of " all those who were engaged in propagating Christianity ") who baptized " his own disciple," and that disciple *in the first century*, is evidently a continuation of the Church in the house, or of the relation of a " master of Israel " and " the adoption " of the Old Testament Church. The master of Israel circumcised a landborn (an " adult," as we have seen), following him in " the regenera-

ens, "*your*" *children;* "And if children, then heirs (with you, an under-shepherd); heirs of God, and joint heirs with Christ" (the chief-shepherd and "messenger of the covenant") and "ye shall make them to inherit among your children after you unto the inheriting (that they may inherit) a possession" (Lev. xxv, 46) in the earthly Canaan, the earthly possession of the Church of God; or, that they may have "an inheritance among them that are sanctified"—the Church.

In reading, with our translators, "Both thy bondmen and thy bondmaids," we not only blot from remembrance *the genealogy* of this most interesting portion of "the family of God," and not only lose the means of understanding the allusions, in the New Testament Scriptures, to the triumphs of that Spirit which moved the prophets to speak for the edification of men under that economy, and not only rob the Master, "the messenger of the covenant," "Jesus Christ the same yesterday and to-day

---

tion," and became his "father in God," or "godfather," and that landborn became his son "in the Lord," or "the adoption," or "the regeneration." This name, "the regeneration," applied to landborns "upon being circumcised after an examination," under the Old Testament dispensation, and applied to "adults," upon being baptized after an examination, under the New Testament dispensation (the person immediately upon being baptized being called "the regeneration") seems to have led some to suppose that the Fathers of the first and second centuries taught the modern doctrine of "baptismal regeneration."

and forever," of the glory of his power as herein manifested; but we *give occasion to the enemy to blaspheme.* Who has not heard the *blasphemous imputation:* " Well, I know slavery is wrong, but it's in the Bible?" Not so; according to the above showing, your *pais* and your *paidiskea* were your young men and your maidens, your sons and your daughters, " the adoption" in a "household of God"—that part of the flock of an under-shepherd, the head of a " household of God," over whom the Holy Ghost gave him oversight, and over whom he " shall not rule with rigor" (Lev. xxv, 46) at the peril of the eternal salvation of his soul. They were such landborns as had " followed" him in " the regeneration," " children of the covenant" (circumcised), lambs of " the flock of an under-shepherd," and not only " children" and " heirs" and " brothers" of the under-shepherd, but "children" and "heirs" and " brothers" of the chief-shepherd, and of the loved ones of the fold, for whom the chief-shepherd gave his life a " ransom," and favors done to whom he receives as done unto himself—" inasmuch as ye have done it unto one of the least of these *my brethren*, ye have done it unto me"—and whom for any one to injure, it were " better for him that a millstone were hanged about his neck, and he were cast into the sea."

Finally, the reader will have observed, that I have not hitherto attempted any explanation of the

expressions rendered " bought for money," or " that
ye buy." I have remarked on page 106, that the
phrases so rendered are technical phrases, " expressive of a relation of one" " brother" to another
" brother" in that nation and commonwealth of
" brothers," and are *never used* to express a relation
of a foreigner, a son of outland, one of the peoples
of the lands or nations, to one of the Jewish nation;
or, in other words, a Jew never " bought" a son of
outland, a foreigner, or a " Gentile" for a "servant"
—the " buying" and " selling" was within the
brotherhood. Now, that the citizens of that commonwealth or nation of brothers whose laws did
not permit one citizen to take " usury" of another,
nor permit one citizen to exact of another " aught
that is lent" in the year of release, nor permit one
to refuse to lend to another " sufficient for his need,"
harboring " the thought in thy wicked heart, saying, the seventh year, the year of release is at hand"
(Deut. xv, 8, 9), bought and sold one another as
" servants," slaves or " bondmen," in any modern
acceptation of these terms, *is utterly inconceivable*.
Before I discuss such a question, I shall wait till
the " accuser" of " the brethren" shall repeat the
charge; wherefore should I so " offend against the
generation of thy children."

It is difficult to speak of the customs of an age so
long past, among a people whose form of government and social habits are unlike anything we have

ever witnessed. I can understand how it was that a convicted felon, that had "nothing," might "be sold for his theft," and be compelled to labor for some one who could supply the means to "make full restitution." (Ex. xxii, 3). I can understand how it was that a man might be said to "sell himself" (his services) as a laborer for a longer or shorter period, and properly enough such a man might be said to have been "bought," although we would use a different term in such a case.

But their modes of thought and the proprieties of that age are not to be judged by the modes of thought and the proprieties of our age. Parents now, in giving daughters in marriage, never expect a "dowry." "Among us, the father usually gives a portion to his daughter, which becomes the property of her husband; but in the east, the bridegroom offers to the father of his bride a sum of money, or value to his satisfaction, before he can expect to receive his daughter in marriage. Of this procedure we have instances from the earliest times. When Jacob had nothing which he could immediately give for a wife he purchased her by his services to her father Laban, Gen. xxix, 18. So we find Shechem offers to pay any value, as a dowry for Dinah, Gen. xxxiv, 12. In this passage is mentioned a distinction still observed in the east: (1) A 'dowry' to the family, as a token of honor, to engage their favorable interest in the desired alliance.

(2) 'A gift' to the bride herself *e. g.*, of jewels and other decorations, a compliment of honor, as Abraham's servant gave to Rebecca." The " dowry of virgins" seems to have been fifty shekels of silver (compare Ex. xxii, 16, 17, and Deut. xxii, 28, 29). The " daughter" said to have been " sold to be a maidservant" on the part of the parents, is said to have been " betrothed" on the part of the person to whom sold; and whether " the master," or lord " betrothed her to himself" or " betrothed her to his son," " If she please not her master," that is, in modern parlance, if they did not choose upon further acquaintance (" After the marriage was contracted, the young people had the privilege of seeing each other, which was not allowed them before ") to consummate the marriage; " then shall he let her be redeemed," but if not redeemed, and he fail to " deal with her after the manner of daughters," attempting to " diminish her food, her raiment, and her duty of marriage" (hinder her rebetrothal), the endowment was forfeited—" if he do not these three unto her, then shall she go out free without money " (Ex. xxi, 7–11). I shall show, hereafter, that a daughter upon being married, or betrothed, ceased to be a member of her father's household, and in the household to which she was transferred she was a " soul bought" (see Lev. xxii, 10–12, page 201). It is evident that marriages in " households of faith " were " only in the Lord" (1 Cor. vii, 39). If the expres-

sion rendered "bought for money," or "that ye buy" refers to an "endowment" instead of reading in Gen. xvii, 13, "the bought with thy money must needs be circumcised," or must needs be in the Lord, we shall read "the endowed with thy money must needs be circumcised," or must needs be in the Lord; and it is a fact well authenticated, that betrothals took place as early as twelve or thirteen years of age, the age at which the Rabbins say that converts might quit their father's house of their own accord, and upon being circumcised or baptized, "those who were their parents were no longer regarded as such after this ceremony." Then "the children of dwellers" (resident foreigners) who do act the "ger with you" (of their own accord) and the children "of their families that are with you which they begat in your land" (Lev. xxv, 45), circumcised and baptized, or "in the Lord," and "endowed of money," and thus introduced in your families, were "your children," and, if not married within the household, to be dealt with "after the manner of" *sons and daughters.*

I suggest another explanation: When persons "make *a singular* vow, the persons shall be for the Lord by thy estimation. And thy estimation shall be for the male from twenty years old, even unto sixty years old, even thy estimation shall be fifty shekels of silver, after the shekel of the sanctuary. And if it be a female, then thy estimation shall be thirty

shekels of silver. And if it be from five years old even unto twenty years old, then thy estimation shall be of the male twenty shekels, and of the female ten shekels," etc. (Lev. xxvii, 2–8).

A landborn in forsaking father and mother and "following" a master of Israel "in the regeneration" *consecrated himself to God;* or, as we would say of such an one, "the vows of God are upon him." Such a person in becoming a member of a "household of God" took upon him a "vow" to "be for the Lord," in the highest sense of that term, as we understand it. If this be the meaning of a "singular vow" (individual consecration), then we would expect to find, in this connection, references to "the estimation" of "silver." The expression rendered, "bought with money" or "gotten with silver," would supply that reference. Supposing this to be the reference, *the group of facts are very suggestive.* God appoints, or "estimates," the value of a soul, or a life, in "corruptible things"—in so many shekels of "silver." A master of Israel, an under-shepherd, a type of Jesus Christ the great Redeemer, pays in "corruptible things" the set "price" of a soul, and that soul is redeemed and introduced, as his son and his heir, in his household, or "among them that are sanctified," receiving in the corruptible inheritance of the Church (the earthly Canaan) "an inheritance" corruptible, liable to be defiled, and that fadeth away.

What a shadow! As did the under-shepherd so does the chief-shepherd, as did the typical Redeemer so does the antitypical Redeemer. God appointed "the price;" the chief-shepherd, the great Redeemer, pays the appointed "price," "not with corruptible things, such as silver and gold . . . but with his own precious blood" (1 Pet. i, 18, 19). The soul redeemed is introduced as a "son" and "heir" among them that are sanctified (the Church), receiving, in the incorruptible inheritance of the Church (the heavenly Canaan), "an inheritance incorruptible, undefiled and that fadeth not away!" In this view, a landborn, in following a master of Israel in the regeneration, *forsook all* for a home in a "household of God," the household of his typical Redeemer,* and was "saved in hope;" so we forsake all for

---

* The names given to the "master of Israel" favors this view—*"Prince, Master, Lord or Ruler.* All these titles are used—sometimes the one and sometimes the other—to express the authority of the Elders. Isaac, when he instals Jacob in the birthright, says, 'be lord over thy brethren, and let thy mother's sons bow down to thee.' When he tells Esau what he had done, he says, 'I have made him thy lord, and all his brethren have I given to him for servants.' "
" He was all that was implied in the titles Kinsman, *Redeemer*, Revenger or Avenger of blood." " From the first promise of a Saviour, down to the giving of the law at Sinai, he was the *heir of the inheritance*—he was *the Prince* or *Ruler*—he was *the sacrificer or Priest over all his father's house* . . . Hence, every elder brother was a type of Him who is called *the heir of all things—the King—the Prophet—the Great High Priest over all the family of God*" (*Life of Abraham*, by Rev. S. Crothers, D. D., pages 16, 17, 18). From " the giving of

Christ and a home in the household of our redeemer, and are "saved in hope," in that home which he has gone "to prepare" for us, "that house not made with hands eternal in the heavens."

---

the law at Sinai" to the coming of Christ, the elders, of course, ceased to act as Priests, the duties of a priest being performed by the Levites.

It may not be out of place, here, to observe that the phrase rendered "master of Israel," means rather *Teacher of Israel*. Nicodemus says to the Saviour, "we know that thou art a *teacher* (*didaskalos*) come from God" (John iii, 2), and the Saviour says to Nicodemus, "Art thou a master (*didaskalos*—teacher) of Israel" (John iii, 10)? If Nicodemus was one of the *Sanhedrim*, as some have supposed from the expression, "ruler of the Jews" (John iii, 1), it only assures us that he was an elder, teacher, or "master of Israel," or the head of a household of "the people of the congregation." "And the Lord said unto Moses, gather unto me seventy men of the *elders of Israel*, whom thou knowest to be *elders of the people*, and officers over them" (Num. xi, 16), and Moses, having done so, "the Lord took of the Spirit that was upon him and gave it unto the seventy Elders, and it came to pass, that when the spirit rested upon them they prophesied and did not cease" (Num. xi, 24, 25). If he held this high office, then most certainly he was a "master of Israel," or head of a household of "the people of the congregation ;" and this higher office did not interfere with his *first duty*—" to provide for his own household." Noah was an elder and a "preacher of righteousness." The masters or "teachers of Israel," were "preachers of righteousness," and each had charge of a portion of "the heritage of God," or, as under-shepherds of the chief-shepherd, had charge of a portion of "the flock of God "—*their own households*. It was their duty to receive landborns as children into their households and to a seat at the passover table ("when thou hast circumcised him then shall he eat thereof," Ex. xii, 44)

We would then understand Gen. xvii, 13, 14, somewhat as follows: "He that is born in thine house and he that hath consecrated himself to God ('gotten' of the Spirit and the redemption of 'silver') in thine house, or he that will take upon him the vows of God in a household of God, must needs be circumcised, and my covenant shall be in your flesh for an everlasting covenant. And the uncircumcised male whose flesh of his foreskin is not circumcised, that soul shall be cut off (*min*) from his people ('people of the congregation'); he hath broken my covenant." That this is the meaning of the expression rendered, "bought with money" or "gotten of silver," and that this was "the price" for which a landborn, following a master of Israel in the regeneration, was "bought" by that master of Israel—that head of a "household of God" and

---

and answer questions proposed by these children ("when your children shall say unto you, what mean you by this service? Then ye shall say," etc. Ex. xii, 26, 27) and "train these children up in the nurture and admonition of the Lord." So the apostle Peter was an elder, under-shepherd, teacher or "preacher of righteousness," "The *elders* which are among you I exhort, who am also an *elder* ... feed (teach or preach to) the flock of God," and "when the chief-shepherd shall appear ye shall receive a crown of glory" (1 Pet. v, 1-4); or, "turning many *to righteousness*," they shall be "as stars in your crown of rejoicing." The title, *redeemer*, of course, ceased to be applicable to an elder after the coming of Christ; just as the title priest had ceased to be applicable to such, from "the giving of the law at Sinai."

type of the great Redeemer, *I do not assert positively.* While it has the ring of "silver" (an emblem of purity), it becomes us to tread lightly in dealing with things so sacred. With these suggestions, therefore, and with the positions heretofore taken, as to the utter impossibility of the expressions rendered "bought with money" or "that ye buy," being understood in any modern acceptation of these terms, I leave open, for the present, the question or questions, as to the exact purpose or purposes, which money served in connection with transactions between one "brother" and another "brother," in that nation and commonwealth of "brothers;" and, especially, as to the exact purpose or purposes which it served within that inner circle, "the Church of the living God," in connection with a relation existing, or about to exist, between the shepherd and his flock, between the head of a "household of God" and the "children of the covenant," "the regeneration" or "the adoption," in that household.

CHAPTER V.

HOUSEHOLDS OF GOD.

1. And the Lord spake unto Moses, saying,

2. Speak unto Aaron and his sons, that they separate themselves from the holy things of the children of Israel, and that they profane not my holy name, etc.

9. They shall therefore keep mine ordinance, lest they bear sin for it, and die, therefore, if they profane it; I the Lord do sanctify them.

10. There shall no stranger (*zar*) eat of the holy thing; a sojourner (*toshabh*, Heb.—*paroikos*, Sept.—dweller, resident foreigner) of the priest, or a hired servant (hireling), shall not eat of the holy thing.

11. But if the priest buy any soul with his money, he shall eat of it, and he that is born in his house; they shall eat of his meat.

12. If the priest's daughter also be married unto a stranger (*zar*), she may not eat of an offering of the holy things.

13. But if the priest's daughter be a widow, or divorced, and have no child, and is returned unto her father's house, as in her youth, she shall eat of her father's meat; but there shall no stranger (*zar*) eat thereof (Lev. xxii).

I. The priest's household consisted of a "soul" bought "with his money" and "he that is born in his house"—"they shall eat of his meat" (v. 10). Except (1) *when* "*unclean*," "The soul which hath touched any such ('whereby he may be made unclean,' 5th verse) shall be unclean until even, and shall not eat of the holy things, unless he wash his flesh in water. And when the sun is down, he shall be clean, and shall afterward eat of the holy things; because it is his food" (vs. 6–7). Except (2) *when* "*cut off from my* (God's) *presence*." "Say unto them, whosoever he be *of all your seed* ('the born in his house' and the 'soul' bought 'with his money') among your generations, that goeth unto the holy things, which the children of Israel hallow unto the Lord, *having his uncleanness upon him*, that soul shall be *cut off from my presence*" (v. 3). That is, "they shall not come near (*again*) to me to do the office of a priest unto me, nor come near (*again*) to any of my holy things in the most holy place;" "but they shall be (or may be again) ministers in my sanctuary, *having charge at the gates of the house and ministering to the house:* they (those who repent and again exercise the office of a Levite) shall slay the burnt-offering and the sacrifice for the people and they shall stand before them to minister unto them." "But the priests, the Levites, the sons of Zadok, that kept the charge of my sanctuary when the children of Israel went astray from me, they shall

come near to me to minister unto me, and they shall stand before me to offer unto me the fat and the blood, saith the Lord God: *They shall enter into my sanctuary, and they shall come near to my table, to minister unto me and they shall keep my charge"* (See Ez. xliv, 10–16).

The priest's daughter, when married (if married unto a stranger—*a zar*) was no longer of her father's household—"she may not eat of an offering of the holy things" (v. 12). Of course, if she was married to a "soul" bought, or "endowed," "with his (her father's) money," as was the daughter of Sheshan (see 1 Chron. ii, 35–41), she continued *with him* to "eat of it" (v. 11). But if "the priest's daughter be a widow, or divorced (rather 'betrothed' and 'endowed' and not 'pleasing her lord,' had been 'redeemed,' etc., see page 192) and have (if a widow) no child, and is returned unto her father's house, as in her youth, she shall eat of her father's meat; but there shall no stranger (*zar*) eat thereof" (v. 13). The question may be asked, if *the household* consisted of a "soul" bought, or endowed, "with money" and "the born in the house," under which expression would the priest's daughter be designated when in the household of her late husband or father-in-law? I answer, not under the expression "born in his house," but under the expression bought, or endowed, "with his money." So also, if she had been transferred to the household as a

betrothed, she would be designated as one bought, or endowed, "with money;" and whether the head of that household had "betrothed her to himself," or "betrothed her unto his son," "if she pleased not her master," or Lord, the marriage would not be consummated, and "then shall he let her be redeemed," or, not "dealing with her after the manner of daughters," she was at liberty to return to her father's house, "as in her youth," and again eat "of her father's meat," and, of course, was a *zar*, or "stranger," in relation to the household in which lately she had been a "soul" bought, or endowed, "with money." In general, then, a daughter, upon being married, or "betrothed" and endowed, ceased to be a member of her father's household, and in the household to which she was transferred was a "soul" bought, or endowed "with money." Then the expression, "There shall no stranger (*zar*) eat of the holy thing," in the 10th verse, and repeated in the 13th verse, is equivalent to saying that *one of another household* * shall not eat of it.

---

* This meaning of the Hebrew word, *zar*, may be abundantly verified. Thus: "If brethren dwell together, and one of them die, and have no child, the wife of the dead shall not marry without unto a *stranger* (*zar*—one of another household or family); her husband's brother shall go in unto her and take her to him to wife," etc. (Deut. xxv, 5-10). The Sadducees quote this Scripture to make a point against the doctrine of the resurrection, saying, "Master,

Then the priest's household consisted of those who ate the holy meat, viz.: the "soul" bought, or endowed, or redeemed, "with his money," and the

---

Moses said if a man die, having no children, his brother shall marry his wife and raise up seed unto his brother.... Therefore in the resurrection whose wife shall she be of the seven?" (See Matt. xxii, 23-28). It is said of the two women who came before Solomon for judgment as to whom belonged the living child, "And the one woman said, I and this woman dwell in one house ... and we were together; there was no *stranger* (*zar*—one of another house—Sept., *no one*) save we two in the house" (1 Kings iii, 16-18). Eleazer the priest took the brazen censers, which the rebellious Korah and his company had used, and "made broad plates for a covering of the altar, to be a memorial unto the children of Israel that no *stranger* (*zar*—one of another household or family), which is not of the seed of Aaron, come near to offer incense before the Lord; that he be not as Korah and his company" (Num. xvi, 39, 40). Comparing Num. xvi, 1, with the above, it appears that "Korah, the son of Izhar, the son of Kohath, the son of Levi," was a *zar* "which is not of the seed of Aaron." "And thou shalt make it an oil of holy ointment ... And thou shalt anoint Aaron and his sons ... Whoso compoundeth any like it, or whosoever putteth any of it upon a stranger (*zar*—one of another household or family), shall even be cut off from his people" (Ex. xxx, 25, 30, 33). Strange incense and strange fire is always *zarah* incense and *zarah* fire. The "stranger (*zar*) that cometh nigh shall be put to death" (Num. i, 51, and iii, 10, 38). I think the statement to be correct, that every family and household of the Hebrew nation were *strangers* (*zar* or *zarim*) in relation to every other family and household, and of course they were all *brethren in a national sense;* but the prophets say that the *zarim* (brothers) *often acted badly,* "For *strangers* (false brethren) are risen up against me and oppressors seek after my soul, they have not set God before them. Selah" (Ps. liv, 3). "Our *inheritance* is

"born in his house;" and they *are always referred to elsewhere in the Scriptures as his children*—"thy sons," "thy daughters," and "thy seed." Thus we read, "this is thine; the heave offering of their gift, with all the wave offerings of the children of Israel, I have given them unto thee, and to *thy sons* and to *thy daughters* with thee by a statute forever; every one that is *clean* in thy house shall eat of it." "And whatsoever is first ripe in the land, which they shall

---

turned to *strangers* (false or apostate brethren) our houses to foreigners" (Lam. v, 1). "Behold, therefore, I will bring *strangers* (false brethren) upon thee, *the terrible of the nations*"—intestine war (Ez. xxviii, 7). "And strangers (false brethren), the terrible of the nations, have cut him off and have left him ... and all *the peoples* of the earth have gone down from his shadow" (Ez. xxxi, 12). "Your country is desolate, your cities are burned with fire; your land, *strangers* (false brethren) devour it in your presence, and it is desolate as overthrown by *strangers* (false brethren—*guerrillas!*). And the daughter of Zion is left as a cottage in a vineyard, as a lodge in a garden of cucumbers, *as a besieged city*" (Isa, i, 7, 8). Dr. Paley has remarked that it does not appear that the apostle Paul was ever set upon by the Gentiles, unless they were first stirred up by the Jews, except in two instances. The persecutors of King David were the *zarim*, and they are often associated with foreigners (see Chart, right hand column, pages 84, 88). Gesenius, in his Hebrew Lexicon, defines the word *zar*, to mean a "foreigner, one of another nation, not an Israelite;" just the opposite seems to be correct. A clear understanding of the meaning of this word, as used in the prophecies, is all-important to the Bible student. That it is not a synonym of any other word rendered "stranger" in the Bible is very apparent, but we must forbear.

bring unto the Lord, shall be thine; every one that is *clean* in thine house shall eat of it." "All the heave offerings of the holy things which the children of Israel offer unto the Lord have I given *thee and thy sons and thy daughters with thee*, by a statute forever; it is a covenant of salt forever before the Lord unto thee and to *thy seed with thee*." "And ye shall eat it *in every place, ye and your households;*" for it is your reward for your service in the tabernacle of the congregation" (Num. xviii, 11, 13, 19, 31). "And the wave breast and heave shoulder shall ye eat *in a clean place; thou and thy sons and thy daughters with thee*, for they be thy due and thy sons' due, which are given out of the sacrifices of peace offerings of the children of Israel" (Lev. x, 14). There were offerings which "every male shall eat" "in the most holy place" (see Num. xviii, 7–10, and Lev. x, 12, 13, 16–18); but here "every one that is clean in thy house shall eat of it" ("in every place" —"in a clean place") *in any clean place*. We have shown in the previous chapter that those "bought for money," or "that ye buy," were "the adoption" in a "household of God"—were *thy sons and thy daughters*, and not "thy bondmen and thy bondmaids;" so here, the priest and his household are referred to under the expression, "ye and your household;" and we have seen that the priest's household, or those who ate of his meat, consisted of the "soul" bought "with his money" and "the

born in his house;" and this embraced the priest's daughter unless when married, and again and again are those who ate of his meat called "thy sons" and "thy daughters;" and they are called "*thy seed*" ("the children of promise are counted for the seed"); that is, "the regenerate" in a "household of God" are called *children*, just as those in the priest's household who were *not* "born in his house" are called "children" and "thy seed" —"counted" or reckoned as "children" and "thy seed." So in Abraham's household "the adoption," or "the children of the covenant," were Abraham's *seed*, being "of the faith of Abraham." "Thou shalt keep my covenant, therefore, *thou and thy seed after thee in their generations.* This is my covenant which ye shall keep between *me and you and thy seed after thee;* every man child among you shall be circumcised" (Gen. xvii, 9, 10). That is, "thy seed" as defined in the 13th verse: "Every man child (or male) in your generations shall be circumcised," as well "thy seed," "born in the house," as "the adoption," or "thy seed" not of "thy seed"—"the descended of a son of outland which is not of thy seed."

"A dweller (resident foreigner) of the priest and a hireling shall not eat of the holy thing" (v. 10). These did not belong to the priest's household; nor did they belong to any household of "the people of the congregation." "A dweller (resident foreigner)

and hireling shall not eat of it" (the passover, Ex. xii, 45). We shall speak of *the dweller* (resident foreigner) and *hireling* hereafter; and now pass immediately to speak of " households of God" in general.

II. Households of "the people of the congregation" of other tribes, as did the households of the Levites, or priests, consisted of the " born in thy house" and the " bought with thy money," as they "*must needs be circumcised*" (Gen. xvii, 13). It is altogether probable that a daughter, upon being married, ceased to be a member of her father's household, as did the daughter of the priest, as before seen; and under similar circumstances " returned unto her father's house, as in her youth," and was no longer a *stranger* (*zar*) in her father's household.

1. *The " born in the house.*" The children of parents, the heads of a household of " the people of the congregation," were dedicated to God *in infancy*: " And he that is eight days old among you shall be circumcised" (Gen. xvii, 12); so, " when eight days were accomplished for the circumcising of the child, (*paidion*) his name was called Jesus" (Luke ii, 22); and "on the eighth day they came to circumcise the child (*paidion*—infant), and they called him Zaccharias, after the name of his father. And his mother answered, not so," etc. (Luke i, 59, 60). "And in the eighth day the flesh of his foreskin shall be circum-

cised" (Lev. xii, 13). But we read, "when the days of her (Mary's) purification, according to the law of Moses, were accomplished, they brought him to Jerusalem to present him to the Lord;" and "when the parents brought in ('into the temple' where Simeon came and 'took him up') the child (*paidion*)—infant Jesus, *to do for him after the custom of the law*," etc. (Luke ii, 22, 27). Now, observe: A mother might "not come into the sanctuary" and "present" her infant offspring "to the Lord," "until the days of her purifying be fulfilled"—until her infant child was from one and a half to three months old, according as it was a *male or a female* (see Num. xii, 4). But "when the days of her purification were accomplished" (Luke ii, 22) or "when the days of her purifying are fulfilled for a son or a daughter, she shall bring a lamb of the first year for a burnt-offering, and a young pigeon or a turtle-dove, for a sin-offering, unto the door of the tabernacle of the congregation, unto the priest, who shall offer it before the Lord and make an atonement for *her . . . and she shall be clean*" (Num. xii, 6-8). It was when this was done that "the *parents* of Jesus came into the temple," or "into the sanctuary" (Num. xii, 4), and made their first "presentation" of their infant offspring "to the Lord" in his sanctuary, and did "*for him* after the custom of the law"—dedicated him to God, in baptism, as it would seem. "The baptizing of infants was a thing

as well known in the Church of the Jews as ever it hath been in the Christian Church." (Dr. Lightfoot.) This presentation of children for baptism in the sanctuary among the Jews in later times, seems to have occurred at their first visit to the temple, after the child was of proper age, and perhaps generally at, or immediately prior to, their annual feasts. We read, that in the second and third centuries, baptisms were publicly administered twice a year, at Easter and Whitsuntide" (*paschatis et pentecostibus diebus*). These are the days which the early Christians observed as anniversaries of the gathering of the Jews to the temple to keep the feast of the passover and the feast commemorative of the giving of the law, the latter being also the anniversary of the outpouring of the Spirit (Acts ii, 1). Tertullian, who lived near the beginning of the third century, attempts to dissuade parents from "exhibiting such haste to have their infants baptized;" and Fidus, a country pastor, proposed to a council of sixty bishops, who met, A. D., 253, the question, "whether an infant might be baptized before it was eight days old." I think it evident that the early Church, in selecting these days for the administration of the ordinance of baptism, followed the example of the Church under the former dispensation.

2. The "*bought with money*," the landborn born again, "*thy seed*" not of "*thy seed*," or "*the adoption*." These

were adult professors, as we have often seen, and we simply note the fact, often referred to heretofore, that a son of *thirteen* years and a daughter of *twelve* were considered of suitable age to act for themselves in making this profession. Dr. Cannon observes, quoting the Gemara, and Maimonides, a celebrated Rabbi of the twelfth century, that it was "a fixed custom to circumcise and baptize the children of proselytes (*prosēlutoi*) received into the Church;" and "they baptized, as infants, the males under thirteen and females under twelve." That is, "And when a landborn (*prosēlutos*) shall be born again and will keep the passover to the Lord, let all his males (under thirteen years) be circumcised, and (having baptized these males and females, under twelve) then let him come near and keep it," etc. Children over this age, then, were not baptized, as infants but as adults upon profession. We read, that "the parents brought in the child (*paidion*—infant) Jesus to do for him after the custom of the law" (Luke ii, 27), and we read again: "Now his parents went to Jerusalem *every year* at the feast of the passover. And when *he was twelve years old they went up after the custom of the feast.* And when they had fulfilled the days, as they returned the child (*pais*—rendered "young man," Acts xx, 12) Jesus tarried behind in Jerusalem" (Luke xxiv, 43). I think an examination of Greek usage will satisfy any one that the *infant* Jesus which his "parents

brought into" the temple was now the *young man* Jesus; and this language seems to be designed to tell us, not only that the parents of the infant Jesus " presented him to the Lord" "in his sanctuary" in baptism, " according to the custom of the law ;" and that they attended " the passover every year," fulfilling all righteousness, but that Jesus himself was prompt to " fulfill all righteousness," and therefore at " the age of twelve," " after the custom of the feast," as any other well instructed child, " he went up to Jerusalem " and assumed, as one of mature years, the active performance of the duties of a child of the covenant; or, as they would say in ordinary cases, by the blessing of God upon his training, he was ready to " follow " his parents, the heads of a "household of God," " in the regeneration," and was now a *pais*, or "*your pais*," just as " the adoption " was "*your pais*" (Lev. xxv, 44), and the relation now was rather that of the shepherd and his flock. If one of the age of twelve refused to enter upon the active duties of a child of the covenant and observe the passover, the law required that he should be held as unclean, or suspended, from the Church. " The man that is clean and is not in a journey, and forbeareth to keep the passover, even the same soul shall be cut off from (*min*) his people " (" people of the congregation," Num. ix, 13). If children were permitted to act for themselves at this age, it follows that any child of a family of

"the people of the congregation," if he chose at this age so to do, could "forsake his father and mother" and their religion, and make his home in any family of "the people of the land," and put himself beyond the government and instruction of an under-shepherd of the great shepherd of Israel; but not so the (*pais*) "young man" Jesus; he continued with his parents and "*was subject unto them*" (Luke ii, 51)—"subject unto his parents as the heads of "a household of God; and, as "your *pais*," (Lev. xxv, 44) these parents must not "*rule over him with rigor*" (Lev. xxv, 46).

We read, that "when they (his parents) had performed all things according to the law (in the temple where they had brought the infant Jesus 'to do for him according to the custom of the law') of the Lord, they returned unto Gallilee to their own city Nazareth. And the child (*paidion*—infant) Jesus grew, and waxed strong in spirit, filled with wisdom, and the grace of God was upon him" (Luke ii, 39, 40). But after he was "twelve years old," and was called the "young man (*pais*) Jesus" (vs. 42, 43), we read, "And Jesus increased in wisdom and stature (in the margin—age) and in favor with God and man" (Luke ii, 52), and this completed the history of the (*pais*) *young man* Jesus until he was thirty years of age and entered upon his public ministry, when he was no longer the (*pais*) young man Jesus; or, as the word is usually rendered, the

servant Jesus, and was no longer "subject" unto his parents. I think the conclusion is warranted, that the children of a family of "the people of the congregation," upon arriving at twelve and thirteen years of age, were expected to enter upon the active discharge of the duties of a child of the covenant; and that neglecting these duties, were cut off from "the people of the congregation," or were "suspended," or separated as unclean.

3. A dweller (resident foreigner) and a hireling shall not eat of it (the passover, Ex. xii, 45). We have seen that "A dweller (resident foreigner) of the priest or a hireling shall not eat of the holy thing" (Lev. xxii, 10)—formed no part of the priest's household.

(1) *The hireling:* From the fact that the relation of the hireling to the family was only temporary, like the relation of the priest's married daughter to her father's household during a temporary stay in her father's house, the hireling formed no part of a "household of God." They might not eat of the passover (Ex. xii, 45), nor eat of the holy things in the priest's household (Lev. xxii, 10). I know of no evidence going to show that a foreigner ever lived with a family of "the people of the congregation" as a hireling; nor does it seem that one *clean*, or a member of the Jewish Church, ever became a hireling. The internal regulations of the Church in relation to "inheritances" seem to have been so

arranged as to prevent such a thing. The landborns who were "gleaners," and for whose necessities "tithes" were laid up every third year "within thy gates" (Deut. xiv, 28, 29, and xxvi, 11–15) seem, in the main, to have been the hirelings, and while living with the head of such a family as his hirelings ("thy landborn that is in thy camp, from the hewer of thy wood unto the drawer of thy water," Deut. xxix, 11) they were brought directly under the instruction of the head of a "household of God," a shepherd of Israel, or a "preacher of righteousness," and, as we would say, "under the means of grace," and upon conversion, "when thou hast circumcised him" (Ex. xii, 44) ceased to be hirelings and became "the adoption" in a "household of God." (See further, foot note, page 54.)

But, I observe; that a male of "the people of the land" of "the stock of Israel" *might be a hireling*, as above, but *could not become* "the adoption" in a "household of God"—a household of the Hebrew of the Hebrews, or the landborn born again. "If thou buy a Hebrew (Hebrew 'stock,' but not a Hebrew of the Hebrews) servant (*pais*—'young man') six years he shall serve thee; and in the seventh he shall go out free for nothing. If he came in by himself he shall go out by himself; if he were married, then his wife shall go out with him. If his master have given him a wife, and she have borne him sons (*uios*) or daughters, the wife

and her children (*paidia*—infants) shall be her master's, and he shall go out by himself. And if the servant (*pais*—'young man') shall plainly say, I love my master (the head of a 'household of God') my wife and my children (*paidia*—my infants); I will not go out free. Then his master shall bring him to the judges ('the house of judgment' of tradition); he shall also bring him to the door, or unto the door post, and his master shall bore his ear through with an awl, and he shall serve him forever" (Ex. xxi, 2–6)—*unto the jubilee*. Turning to the law relating to the jubilee, we read: "And if thy brother that dwelleth by thee be waxen poor, and be sold (*nimkar*—rendered 'sell himself,' v. 47) unto thee thou shalt not compel him to serve as a bondservant (*oiketees*—every *oiketees*, etc., "shall eat of it"—the passover, Ex. xii, 44). But as a hireling and as a dweller (resident foreigner), he shall be with thee (*i. e.*, not of your household, not of the priest's household—Lev. xxii, 10—not of any household of "the people of the congregation," Ex. xii, 45) and shall serve thee unto the year of the jubilee; and then shall he depart from thee both he and his children (*tekna*) and shall return unto his own family, and unto the possession of his fathers shall he return. For they are my servants (*oiketai*—already of a family and household of God) which I brought forth (or 'redeemed') out of the land of Egypt; they shall not be sold as (*oiketou*) bondmen"

(Lev. xxv, 39–42). They shall not be transferred to your households as "the adoption," or the "redemption of silver," is transferred; since the Lord thy God hath redeemed thee (the seed of Israel) in the land of Egypt (see Deut. xv, 12–15), and ye are my servants (*oiketai*) already. "The adoption" was thy seed not of the seed of Israel (the descended of a son of outland, or the child of a resident foreigner) and, in being adopted into a household of God, became one of the *oiketai* of God, or one of a "household of God" *for the first time*. The one, necessarily, must forsake his father and mother and break off every natural tie before he became an *oiketees*, or a member of a "household of God;" the other was already "my *oiketees*," or "my servant," and therefore "as a hireling and as a dweller (resident foreigner) he shall be with thee, and shall serve thee unto the year of the jubilee. And then shall he depart from thee both he and his children with him, and shall return unto his own family and unto the possession of his fathers shall he return" (Lev. xxv, 40, 41); "for every one of the children of Israel (seed of Israel) shall keep himself to the inheritance of the tribe of his fathers" (Num. xxxvi, 7). The adoption, of course, did not, at the jubilee, "return to the family and possession of his fathers" (a foreign family and possessions or "lands," all of which he had "forsaken") but continued, as we have seen, a permanent addition to the family, and

the tribe of the family, into which he had been adopted. The apostle refers to "the adoption" in a "household of faith," or, as it was called in the first and second centuries, in the house of his "godfather:" "Servants (*oiketai*), be subject to your masters," etc., even to the "froward;" "For ye were as sheep going astray; but (in their households) are returned unto the Shepherd and Bishop of your souls"* (1 Pet. ii, 18, 25)—they have the *care* and *oversight* of your souls.

We note here that the inspired writer enjoins (1), that they shall not "*rule with rigor*" (Lev. xxv, 39, 43) over thy brother living with thee as a hireling and dweller (resident foreigner), or who *was not* of their households; and (2), they shall not "*rule with rigor*" (Lev. xxv, 44–46) over "the adoption" or "your *pais*," an *oiketees*, or one who *was* of their households (ate the passover, Ex. xii, 44); and (3), "if (Lev. xxv, 47–53) a dweller and landborn (resident landborn, or head of a family of 'the people of the land') wax rich by thee, and thy brother

---

* Substantially the same thing exists among modern missionaries. Every reader of missionary periodicals has observed that converts are frequently given the name of some prominent man in the Church at home, such as "Archibald Alexander," "Miller," etc. Such persons are substantially the *oiketai* of the missionary family, or members of the missionary household, over whom the pastor of the missionary Church as a "Shepherd and Bishop," has a *care and oversight*. Bishops may at times be "froward."

that dwelleth by him wax poor, and sell himself unto the landborn a dweller (resident landborn) by thee or to the stock of the landborn's family ... as a yearly hireling shall he be with thee, and the other shall not *rule with rigor over him* in thy sight."

(2) *A dweller* (resident foreigner): The dweller (resident foreigner) could not be a member of a "household of God." They might not eat of the passover (Ex. xii, 45); nor eat of the holy things in the priest's household (Lev. xxii, 10). As we have seen before, they were persons of foreign birth but not of foreign associations, and they seem to have lived with the families of "households of God," and enjoyed much intimacy in such families, but could not be members of the "household." In times past, or under the Old Testament economy, they were "aliens from the commonwealth of Israel and strangers (*xenoi*—guests) from the covenants of promise," but "the middle wall of partition" being broken down, they are no more *xenoi* (guests of the covenants of promise) and dwellers (resident foreigners) but fellow-citizens with the saints and of "the household of God" (Eph. ii, 12-19). The Psalmist says: "Do not I hate them, O Lord, that hate thee?" rather, *Do not I abhor them that abhor thee?* and this seems to be the force of the injunctions, "thou shalt not seek their peace (peoples of the lands) or their wealth forever" (Ez. ix, 11-12); and "thou shalt not seek their peace (a Moabite or

an Ammonite, etc.) nor prosperity all thy days forever" (Deut. xxiii, 3-6). But should any of these "peoples of the lands," etc., renounce their nationality and the associations of image-worshiping nations, and take up their abode within that commonwealth, "join themselves to the Lord," "take hold of his covenant," and "keep his Sabbaths" (Isa. lvi, 6, 7), they were no longer reckoned as belonging to these nations; and, although not enjoying a formal union with the Jewish Church, they were not regarded of them by any means with aversion. The attitude of pious Hebrews toward a pious foreigner, is beautifully expressed in the language of Moses to Hobab: "Come thou with us and we will do thee good; for the Lord hath spoken good concerning Israel" (Num. x, 29). And again, in the language of King David, solicitous, in the midst of his own troubles, for the comfort of Ittai the pious foreigner, the *xenos* or "*xenos* of the covenant of promise," "Wherefore goest thou with us? . . . seeing I go whither I may, return thou and take back thy brethren; *mercy and truth be with thee.*" The expressions of attachment uttered by the pious Ruth to Naomi and her people—"thy people shall be my people, and thy God my God"—is only equaled by the earnest expressions of esteem uttered by Boaz— "all the city of my people doth know that thou art a virtuous woman." Nor was her "forsaking her father and mother and the land of her nativity" to

go unrewarded: "The Lord recompense thy work and a full reward be given thee of the Lord God of Israel, under whose wings thou art come to trust." David himself was accustomed to sing, "the Lord doth build up Jerusalem, he gathereth together the outcasts of Israel," the "escaped of the nations," the "*xenoi* of the covenants of promise," or pious foreigners who were children of "the Jerusalem above, the mother of us all" (the pious of every nation). Indeed, if I mistake not, the law enjoined this kindness toward the "escaped of the nations" as a duty. We read: "Thou shalt not deliver unto his master, the servant (*pais*—'young man') which is escaped ('escaped of the nations') *from* (*min-im*—'departure from,' 'from with,' separating himself from) his master, or Lord, unto thee. He shall dwell (be a 'dweller') with thee even *among thy drawing nigh* (in a family of a 'household of God') in one of thy gates where it liketh him best (is good for him—margin), thou shalt not oppress him" (Deut. xxiii, 15, 16). If I mistake not, the refugee, or the "escaped of the nations," as above, who was to *dwell* (Sept., *katoik.*, rendered "dwellers," Acts ii, 9) *among thy drawing nigh*, or in a family of a "household of God," was *the dweller* (resident foreigner) of the priest's household (Lev. xxii, 10), and the dweller (resident foreigner) of any "household of God," who might not eat the passover with the one, or the holy things with the other; and was there,

not as an *oiketees*, or a member of "the household," but as a *guest* of "the household;" and these guests, or "*xenoi* of the covenants of promise," seem to have lived in the closest intimacy with those to whom belonged the covenants of promise in the fullest sense.

It is true, they were denied a "nearness" of access, in the earthly sanctuary, to the earthly symbols of Jehovah's presence; and, true, they might not possess an "inheritance" in the earthly Canaan; but what did it matter to them, as to these "shadows," if, with the eye of faith, they had a realizing view that "a great multitude, which no man could number, of *all nations, and kindreds, and peoples, and tongues, stood before the throne and before the Lamb!*" What did it matter, if they were entitled to a "nearness" in "the true tabernacle which the Lord pitched and not man"—in the heavenly sanctuary at the foot of the throne, and literally "face to face" with the Lamb! What did it matter to them, if, during this *fleeting* existence they received no "inheritance" in the earthly Canaan, if they had a realizing view that in the heavenly Canaan, "the Jerusalem above, the mother of *us all*," the "redeemed" "out of every kindred, and tongue, and people, and nation," *received* "an inheritance among them that are sanctified"—"an inheritance incorruptible, undefiled, and that fadeth not away!"

I observe here, that the Jewish Church was not

intended to be an embodiment of all the pious of earth, or even of all the pious of the Jewish nation. The deformed Levite "that is broken footed, or broken handed, or crooked backed, or a dwarf, or that hath a blemish in his eyes," etc., might not officiate—" not *come nigh* to offer the bread of his God" (Lev. xxi, 17–21). The prophet pronounces, in the name of the Lord, a blessing upon, and declares that " salvation is near to," not only the son of outland that "keeps his Sabbaths" and "takes hold of his covenant," or becomes a " *xenos* of the covenants of promise;" but also pronounces a blessing upon, and declares that " salvation is near to," the " eunuchs that keep his Sabbaths, and choose the things that please him, and take hold of his covenant," and assures them of an " everlasting name and a place in his house (the upper sanctuary) that shall not be cut off" (Isa. lvi, 1–7); yet the eunuch might not (draw " near ") " enter into the congregation of the Lord" (Deut. xxiii, 1); or, which is the same thing (see Lam. i, 10), might not enter the (earthly) sanctuary. The reason seems to have been that the Jewish Church as an organization had a typical character—those entering the earthly sanctuary were types of those who shall enter the heavenly sanctuary, or of the inhabitants of heaven, of " the general assembly and Church of the firstborn which are written in heaven," of the " one fold," that glorified " Church not *having spot*

or wrinkle or any such thing." Hence, *the deformed* shall not officiate at the altar or enter the earthly sanctuary. The organization of the Jewish Church, therefore, being intended to shadow forth certain great truths respecting the redeemed in heaven, the truly pious of that nation and within that organization, and the truly pious of other nations, and therefore necessarily without that organization, only felt themselves to be separated by the forms of that organization, *but were not separated in spirit or affection.* The developments of Phariseeism are no fit representation of the relations of the one to the other. The bigoted, persecuting spirit of Phariseeism is abundantly illustrated in their conduct. They filled the place " in the temple of God," where pious foreigners worshiped ("the court of the Gentiles," or nations), "with tables of money changers and the seats of them that sold doves;" and made that place, appointed of God as a place of "prayer for all peoples" or "nations," a very "den of thieves." (Compare Matt. xxi, 12, 13, and Isa. lvi, 6, 7). Well might the disciples, contemplating the bold act of "the master of the house" on that occasion, *call to mind* "that it was written, the 'zeal of thine house hath eaten me up.'" They took "the price of blood" to buy the potter's field in which to bury (*xenoi*) pious foreigners. The fond hope of Ruth (the *xenea*) was to find her last resting-place with the pious Naomi: "Where thou diest, will I die, and

there will I be *buried;*" but henceforth these "whited sepulchres," reckoning themselves to be the "special favorites" of heaven, were about to separate from themselves, in sepulture, those with whom they were in no wise worthy to associate in this life. This burying "strangers" "in the potter's field"—outside of "consecrated ground," "clanks" as that "machine" which the head of the great modern apostacy "runs" in our day. These developments of the apostate Jewish Church, ("the Jerusalem that then was, and was in bondage with her children") is no more a fit representation of the true spirit of the Old Testament Church toward pious foreigners, than the spirit of Roman Catholicism is a fit representation of the true spirit of the Gospel.

I see no evidence in Bible history that the Jews were forbidden to marry pious foreigners—the "escaped of the nations" or the "*xenea* of the covenants of promise." There is nothing connected with the history of Boaz and Ruth, going to show that their marriage had not the divine approval. The permission given (Deut. xxi, 12-14) to marry a captive foreigner was on the condition, that she renounce all associations with, and a desire to return to, her kindred—"she shall shave her head and pare her nails, and she shall put the raiment of her captivity from off her, and remain in thine house, and bewail her father and her mother a full month." It

seems to have been, in olden time, "a shame for a woman to be shaven." On condition that this captive foreigner cut off "her glory"—divest herself of her beauty and her pride—and put away the raiment in which she was taken captive, and all evidences that she felt herself a captive; and, after a suitable time, cease to "lament her father and her mother," and give up her desire to return to her kindred; in a word, renounce her people and her kindred, she was then in the family as a betrothed; but, the marriage not being consummated, as referred to heretofore, "thou shalt let her go whither she will" —without that "redemption" which was usual in the case of daughters "betrothed" to be (an *oiketees*) a member of "the household" (see Ex. xxi, 7–11). Solomon sinned in forming alliances, or making "affinity," with foreign families — in marrying women of foreign associations, such as Pharaoh's daughter; and although "he built for her a house out of the city of David, because he would not allow her to dwell in the house of David king of Israel" (2 Chron. viii, 11), "nevertheless even him did *outlandish* (foreign) women cause to sin" (Neh. xiii, 36). These foreign women whom Solomon married "turned away his heart after other gods" (gods whom these women worshiped); but the heart of Ruth was toward "the Lord God of Israel, under whose wings she had come to trust." The children of those who had married foreign wives, in the

times of Nehemiah, "spake half in the speech of Ashdod and could not speak in the Jews' language," hence they were evidently women of *foreign associations*. From this class of foreign wives, or "wives of the peoples of the land," Ezra caused the people to "separate themselves;" but is it not evident that such marriages* as that of Boaz with Ruth, the

---

* Several of the early Christian Fathers seem to think that there is a great mystery hidden in the quarrel of Miriam and Aaron with Moses, "about his marrying a stranger" (see Num. xii, 1). Origen, an eminent Father, born in the year A. D., 185, discourses as follows: "1. Zipporah, a *Cushite*, espoused by *Moses*, evidently points out the choice which Jesus Christ has made of the *Gentiles* for his spouse and Church. 2. The jealousy of Aaron and Miriam against Moses and Zipporah, *signifies* the hatred and envy of the Jews against Christ and his apostles, when they saw that the mysteries of the kingdom of heaven had been opened *to the Gentiles* (nations) of which they had rendered themselves unworthy," etc. Poole, a well-known writer, born in the year A. D., 1624, observes, upon the supposition that a "stranger upon sojourning," etc. (Ex. xii, 48), "was admitted to the same privileges with the Israelites," that Moses " as well as any other, might marry an Ethiopian or an Arabian woman." The language of Origen does not hint at, or admit of, the possibility of such an explanation. Dr. Lardner, born A. D., 1684, has well observed, that " he does not believe that the notion of two sorts of Jewish proselytes can be found in any Christian writer before the fourteenth century or later "—some two hundred years previous to this explanation given above by Poole. In that gloomy period of the history of the Church and the world, seems to have originated the mistake of calling the two sorts of *proselutoi*, or landborns, " two sorts of proselytes."

"*xenea* of the covenants of promise," were looked upon in a different light?

The following positions, then, seem to me to be correct. The inmates of any habitation of "the people of the congregation" consisted, or might consist, of three classes of persons, viz.: Those (1), of the family who were pious, or "the household;" (2), the entire family, parents and children, converted and unconverted, or clean and unclean; and (3), the hirelings and dwellers, or pious foreigners, living in a household of God as guests of "the household." A member of the Jewish Church might marry a pious foreigness, or a "*xenea* of the covenants of promise," and she would become a *member of his family but not of his household*. The clean and unclean of a Jewish family seem to have occupied the same home and mingled together much as the professing and nonprofessing children of any family in modern time; but not so, when they went up to the temple or sanctuary. Thus we read: "thou and *thy household* shall eat the firstling males of thy flock before the Lord thy God, year by year, in the place which the Lord shall choose"—at the temple. But the firstling having an "ill blemish, thou shalt not sacrifice it unto the Lord thy God. Thou shalt eat it *within thy gates* (at home); the clean and the unclean"—*the entire family* "shall eat it alike" (see Deut. xv, 19–23). The comfort of the pious Ruth, if not permitted to eat the passover with her

husband for such a technical reason, would be in no wise incommoded. She might accompany him up to the temple, "year by year," and present her offerings to the Lord in "the court of the *nations*" where it was to be received "from her hand" (Lev. xxii, 25), and offered for her by the priest officiating at the altar; and there she might present her supplications to "the Lord God of Israel, under whose wings she had come to trust;" and there she had the assurance that her "sacrifices should be accepted on his altar," and her prayers, thus offered in that place "of prayer for all peoples" (Isa. v, 6, 7), should be heard; and, although not permitted to "take the children's bread" (Mark vii, 24–30), yet, as the "woman, a Greek, a Syrophenician *by nation*," pleads, she might there, beneath *the overshadowings* of the sanctuary, at least spiritually, "eat the children's crumbs." They both, no doubt, understood well, that this separation in their worship during their visits, "year by year," to "the Jerusalem that now is," was ordered in all wisdom by their heavenly Father; but this to them *was as nothing*, since, "living together as heirs of the grace of life" during this weary pilgrimage, they should soon together enter and together "eat bread" in "the kingdom"—"the Jerusalem above, the mother of *us all!*" *Glorious hope!* We have seen that, on the part of the "master of Israel" and "the adoption," God's approval or "praise" was *the considera-*

tion with which any natural tie must not interfere; and here, for the time being, *a line separated husband and wife!* The lesson, "shadowed" forth, seems to be that *every relation of life is subordinate to our relation to God.* Our attachment to father and mother and wife and children must be subordinate, for "He that loveth *father and mother* more than me is not worthy of me; and he that loveth *son or daughter* more than me is not worthy of me." Our attachment to life itself must be subordinate, for: "If any man come to me, and hate not his father, and mother, and wife, and children, and brethren, and sisters, *yea, and his own life also, he can not be my disciple.*"

To say that a pious foreigner had no interests in "the covenants of promise," would be as far from the truth, as to say that they had full privileges in the Jewish Church, under "the covenants" with Abraham. The true spirit of one toward the other is breathed in that expression of King David to Ittai, the *xenos:* "*Mercy and truth be with thee,*" yet for reasons pertaining to that economy he could only be a dweller (resident foreigner) and (*xenos*) "guest of the covenants of promise" in the priest's household or in any household of "the people of the congregation"—*not* a "fellow-citizen with the saints," *nor* "of the household of God."

APPENDIX.

A.—Proposed Rendering of Ex. xii, 43–49.

As an example of the changes which the author would propose in the rendering of the Scriptures called in question in the foregoing pages, the following translation of Ex. xii, 43–49 is submitted; any serious departure from which must lead to confusion and error.

(43.) And the Lord said unto Moses and Aaron, This is the ordinance of the passover; any son of outland shall not eat thereof. (44.) But every son ("the adoption"—*oiketees*, member of "the household") of a man (the head of a household of "the people of the congregation") bought ("gotten," or "redeemed," etc.) for money, when thou hast circumcised him then shall he eat thereof. (45.) A dweller (resident foreigner) shall not eat thereof. (46.) In one house shall it be eaten; thou shalt not carry forth aught of the flesh abroad out of the house; neither shall ye break a bone thereof. (47.) All the congregation of Israel shall keep it. (48.) And when a landborn shall be born again with thee and will keep the passover to the Lord, let all his males be circumcised, and then let him come near and keep it, and he shall be as the Hebrew of the Hebrews of the land, for no uncircumcised (landborn) shall eat thereof. (49.) One law shall be to the ("people of the congregation") Hebrew of the Hebrews and to the landborn born again among you.

Instead of reading, as in our translation: "There shall no stranger eat thereof" (v. 43), "A foreigner," etc., "shall not eat thereof" (v. 45), "And when a stranger shall sojourn," etc.,

"then shall he eat thereof" (v. 48), we would read: "Any son of outland (of foreign birth and associations) shall not eat thereof" (v. 43), "A dweller (resident foreigner, or not of foreign associations)," etc., "shall not eat thereof" (v. 45), "And when a landborn" (one born in the land, and associated with the Jewish nation, in national obligations) "shall be born again," etc., "then let him come near and keep it" (v. 48).

B.—The Two Covenants.

Viewed from our standpoint, there seem to have been "two covenants;" the one, written "with ink" "in tables of stone," and of a carnal nature; the other, unwritten (or written "with the Spirit of the living God" "in fleshly tables of the heart," and known by a sign—" the token of the covenant in your flesh") and of a spiritual nature; and connected with the keeping of either there were pledges of "life," but "life" in different senses.

(1.) *The covenant with the civil Israel, or "the people of the land."* The being born in the land and a willingness to take an oath binding the person, in respect to God and "the people of the land," to perform all the duties of a citizen ("*his* covenant which he *commanded you* to perform, even the *ten commandments*"—Deut. iv, 13) were the conditions required of candidates for citizenship; and "the people of the land," or citizens of the commonwealth, were required to see that this oath was observed; and the man observing it was entitled to his reward, that is, to "life," but to "life," as connected with "the commandment with promise," even *length of days* "in the land which the Lord thy God giveth thee;" but the man *not* observing this covenant—in so far as it said "*thou shalt not*"—*had no such promise.* We have shown heretofore that any one of "the people of the land" violating the ten commandments in their negative requirements—in the

sense pointed out—*were to be punished with death* by "the people of the land."

(2.) *The covenant with the spiritual Israel, or "the people of the congregation."* A professed new birth on the part of one born in the land and a willingness to take another oath (the oath of the covenant of circumcision) binding the person, in respect to God and "the people of the congregation," to perform the duties of a member of the congregation, were the conditions required of candidates for membership in the congregation; and "the people of the congregation" were required to see that this oath was observed; and the man observing it was entitled to the promises of the covenant of circumcision—the promises to the regenerate, to the man "born again" that he shall "see the kingdom of God." The man "doing this" was "saved in hope," or was to be adjudged by "the people of the congregation" as having "eternal life;" and the man *not* doing this (not performing the duties of a member of the congregation) was to be adjudged by "the people of the congregation," as no longer entitled to entertain such a hope. In respect, therefore, to each of these covenants, it was strictly true that the "man that doeth these things shall live in them;" but in one case the "life" promised was "length of days," in the other "eternal life."

This use of "the same word (life) in two senses, or rather, in a higher and lower application of the same sense," seems to be the foundation of that "extraordinary dictum" contained in Mark viii, 35, which Alexander, in his commentary, paraphrases thus: " *Whosoever will* (is willing, wishes to) *save his life* (*i. e.*, his natural life, or the life of his body for its own sake, as the highest good to be secured or sought) *will* (by that very act not only lose but) *destroy it.*" That is, he who kept the law in so far as it said " *thou shalt not,*" enjoyed all that was promised to such observers—civil protection in the commonwealth of Israel and "length of days," as we have seen—but by "refusing to look higher, he forfeited life in heaven;" but whosoever kept the spiritual covenant, regardless of every *earthly consideration,* such as "father and mother," etc., or " *Whosoever loses or destroys* (*i. e.*, allows to

be destroyed, if needful) *his life* (in the lower sense, before explained) *for my sake* (in my service and at my command) *he shall save his life by losing it*, or only lose it in a lower sense to save it in the highest sense conceivable."

The Apostle refers to these "two covenants" (Gal. iv, 24) as (1) "the covenant which was confirmed before of God in Christ," and (2) "the law which was four hundred and thirty years after" (Gal. iii, 17), or as in Deut. iv, 13, "his covenant even the ten commandments, which he wrote upon two tables of stone." Now, "the inheritance," the Apostle says, was not of the *written* covenant, or the law, but of the *unwritten*: "For if *the inheritance* be of the law, it is no more of promise; but God gave it to Abraham by promise" (Gal. iii, 18). That is, as we have seen, an entire family of landborns, or an individual landborn, each upon being born again and circumcised received "an inheritance," the one within a tribe (see pages 152, 153), the other (see pages 153—160) within a family. The obligation of the carnal covenant or the law was assumed (if not formally, impliedly) prior to this, in assuming the duties of "the people of the land;" but there was no "inheritance" connected with this assumption of the duties of a citizen.

These "two covenants" seem to have been essentially the same—the written being "added" to the unwritten "because of transgressions" (Gal. iii, 19). That is, the addition was not made out of regard to any deficiency in the first covenant, but out of regard to "transgressions," or man's weakness. The written neither "added to" nor "disannulled" (Gal. iv, 15) any promise contained in the unwritten—all was implied in the first covenant that was contained in the second. The written covenant, carnal covenant, or the law, *marked out* (what was well understood, but in danger of being lost sight of through the multiplication of "transgressions") the foundations of civil society, the fundamental law of "the commonwealth"—*if you will exist as a nation these ten commandments* "*thou shalt not*" break. Of course, there were no temporal penalties connected with the keeping of the spiritual covenant—a covenant only kept in the affections. The

language of the spiritual Israel to the man violating the laws of God's house, was simply, "you have no part nor lot in this matter," or *depart from us* (separated from the *clean*); but when the conduct of that man, or any other man of "the people of the land," struck at the foundations of civil society—where he was guilty of a high-handed breach of the ten commandments, *then was aimed at him that thunderbolt, thou shalt die.*

But, as we have said, these "two covenants" seem to have been essentially the same covenant, or the one so much of an amplification of the other, that we can only speak of them as the same covenant, connected with the keeping of which there were promises of "life," but life in different senses, according as this covenant was kept in "the letter," or in "the letter" and "spirit." In relation to the *higher* "life," the observing the covenant, or the law given on Sinai, only in "the letter" (in so far as it said "thou shalt not") "genders to bondage"—begets in such observers "a certain fearful looking for of judgment" (such are still under the bondage of sin and Satan, as opposed to that freedom wherewith Christ makes his people free) and "worketh wrath," or leads to separation from God and eternal ruin. But the observing the law in "the letter" and in "the spirit" "giveth life"—begat a cheerful hope in view of the judgment (brings such to that freedom wherewith Christ makes his people free, as opposed to the bondage of sin and Satan), and as thus observed, the law, "ordained to life," "gave life," eternal "life," and joys at God's right hand.

The earthly Jerusalem seems to have been a miniature representation of "the Jerusalem above, the mother of us all" (pious Jew and "Gentile"), and the spiritual Israel a type of the inhabitants of "the Jerusalem above"—of that great company there gathered, "born again, not of corruptible seed, but of incorruptible, by the word of God, which liveth and abideth forever." The Jewish Church had, in Paul's time, ceased to be a spiritual Church (the "Jerusalem which now is, is in bondage—to sin—with her children"), and, therefore, was no longer a fit representation of the true Church,

for the "Jerusalem which is above *is free*" in the freedom of those "born again not of corruptible seed," or in that freedom wherewith Christ makes his people free. So Ishmael, entering upon the duties of a child of the covenant at the age of "thirteen years" (Gen. xvii, 25), subsequently "mocked" and gave evidence that he was unregenerate or under bondage to sin—"he that was born after the flesh persecuted him that was born after the spirit." Hence it was impossible that the "mocking" "persecuting" Ishmael, though the firstborn and legal heir to "the inheritance," *should be heir to this* "*inheritance;*" it having become evident that he was not a type of those in possession of "the inheritance" above. Hence, it was impossible that the apostate "persecuting" Jewish Church of Paul's time, "in bondage (to sin) with her children," or an unregenerate Church, though "the seed of Abraham according to the flesh" and legal heir to "the inheritance," *should be heir to this* "*inheritance,*" it having become evident that she was no longer a type of the Church of the firstborn in possession of "the inheritance" above. Nay, sooner would God "raise up children to Abraham of these stones," than allow such to be heirs of his inheritance! Hence they were "cast out" or "cast away," and, says the Apostle to the Galatians: "Now, we brethren, as Isaac was, are the children of promise."

A few words of a practical character may not here be out of place. The question has been, and may again be asked, what light, if any, does this understanding of the laws of the commonwealth of Israel shed upon the path of duty in the present hour of our own commonwealth? The Hebrew nation were taught to open wide their arms to those born within the limits of the nation ("thou shalt not abhor an Edomite," etc., Deut. xxiii, 7) and to receive them, in subscribing to the fundamental law of the land (the ten commandments), as children of the nation; and they then were entitled to every privilege of citizenship, and the nation was responsible for the conduct of all its citizens. The Ruler of nations appointed them a somewhat different rule of conduct toward those of Moab and Ammon, born in their midst, to put a stamp, as

it were, upon the heartlessness of the children of Lot toward the children of Abraham in not meeting them "with bread and water in the way, when they came forth out of Egypt," etc. (Deut. xxiii, 4). Bating this exception, for which these special reasons were given, evidently the principle was held that, where a man was born, there he was entitled to all the rights of manhood—entitled to them, until by some act aimed at the foundations of civil society, as summed up in the ten commandments, he forfeited them. To this plainest dictate of common sense, no reasoning could add the weight of a feather. In that Book of the living God, which was the guide of that nation, are dotted, on almost every page, warnings to them to beware that they oppress not those born in their midst, but not of their own race. One clear utterance must suffice: "Thou shalt not vex a landborn, nor oppress him; for ye were landborns in the land of Egypt. Ye shall not afflict any widow, or fatherless child. If thou afflict them in any wise, and they cry at all unto me, I will surely hear their cry; and my wrath shall wax hot, and I will kill you with the sword; and your wives shall be widows, and your children shall be fatherless (Ex. xxii, 21–24). Had we as a nation heeded this warning, and not oppressed those born in our land, and by that birth entitled, by the divine law of that commonwealth, to all the rights of manhood, although they were not born of our own Saxon race, there had not been this day around our hearthstones thousands of "wives" made "widows," and tens of thousands of "children" made "fatherless." Where God gives a man breath, there he has appointed to him the rights of manhood; and the nation that contravenes this law will learn sooner or later, by sad experience, that the God of the Hebrews still lives.

www.ingramcontent.com/pod-product-compliance
Lightning Source LLC
Chambersburg PA
CBHW021803230426
43669CB00008B/613